READ THE WORLD

A Country-By-Country Guide
to the Best Books on Africa,
Asia and Latin America

PUSHPINDER KHANEKA

An indispensable guide to the writers, writings, themes and ideas that together provide much-needed insight into a world from which we hear too little. – Gary Younge, author of *Dispatches From the Diaspora*

I have often said, if you want to know a country, read its writers. To know the stories of a country is to discover how the people of a country see themselves, remember and reflect upon their history, consider their present and envision their future. Stories are the key to a nation's sensibility. *Read the World* is the place to start that journey. – Aminatta Forna, author of *Happiness*

A poignant novel, chatty memoir or vivid nonfiction account opens up a society and culture as no media article or academic thesis ever does, making what once seemed baffling suddenly comprehensible. This is the writer's super power: the ability to connect minds halfway across the world from one another. *Read the World* does us all a great service by identifying the books offering those blinding moments of insight into what hitherto seemed impenetrable. – Michela Wrong, author of *Do Not Disturb*

A literary tour that introduces you to the variety of texts available in the larger world of books. A very entertaining read. – Nuruddin Farah, author of *North of Dawn*

What a brilliant idea, and how wonderfully executed. A book packed with great ideas – some familiar, others almost certainly not. A superb set of suggestions for finding powerful writing from all over the world. – Steve Crawshaw, former UK director of Human Rights Watch and author of *Prosecuting the Powerful: War Crimes and the Battle for Justice*

Read the World is like a well-curated travel bookshop, full of surprises and unexpected pleasures. Even if you're not planning a visit, this selection opens the door to the majority world, too often ignored in daily headlines. Every page is full of the smells, sights and sounds of adventures yet to take. – David Loyn, former BBC foreign correspondent and author of *The Long War: The Inside Story of America in Afghanistan Since 9/11*

For anyone interested in these countries here is a portal to the books that explain them. A compact, invaluable guide to novels, fables, reportage and histories, some famous, some overlooked, and all here. – Rory Carroll, author of *Comandante and Killing Thatcher*

A tour de force of the global south, offering a great insight into countries you may want to visit – or steer well clear of. Lots to read, lots that can be learned. – Mike Carter, author of *One Man and His Bike* and *All Together Now*

What a great idea! Exactly what you need on first travelling to a new country. Or even when returning to a familiar one: the depth, nuance and richly complex points of view provided by judiciously chosen fiction and nonfiction. – Aida Edemariam, author of *The Wife's Tale*

Most certainly a labour of literary love, this impressively curated set of books will help you to get to know a vast array of peoples and places. – Ann Wright, translator of Che Guevara's *The Motorcycle Diaries*, and *I, Rigoberta Menchú*

An epic journey through 55 countries around the world, bringing rare insights into the thoughts and feelings of writers and characters too often overlooked – Nick Caistor, former analyst at the BBC World Service

The variety and quality of the titles he has chosen are wonderfully impressive. He certainly knows his books and is incredibly well travelled … You will find some terrific reads chosen by someone who himself has erudition, culture and expertise in the subject of literary wanderlust. – tripfiction.com

A phenomenal achievement. This new edition extends still further over the southern hemisphere. We should be grateful to the author for keeping literature alive and lifting our spirits. – Linda Etchart, Latin America Bureau

Almost as rewarding for considering what you'd have picked for countries you know as it is for countries you don't. *Read the World* can be a gateway to your literary and historical adventures for years to come. – Global Justice Now

Published by Southface Press

Copyright © 2020/2025 Pushpinder Khaneka

ISBN: 978-1-0682036-0-2
eBook: 978-1-0682036-1-9

For my grandmother Karen, who was my window
to the world, and for my mother

About the author

Pushpinder Khaneka is a widely travelled journalist who has worked in Britain and abroad for, among others, the Guardian, the Observer, the Independent, Independent Television News (ITN) and ABC radio. He was deputy editor of the Guardian Weekly from 1994 to 2003, and is author of *Do the Right Things: A Practical Guide to Ethical Living*

I've got a heart like a wheel. Feel like I got to roll – Steve Miller Band

An open book is a mind that speaks; closed, a friend who waits; forgotten, a soul that forgives; destroyed, a heart that weeps – Rabindranath Tagore

Books are the plane, and the train, and the road. They are the destination, and the journey – Anna Quindlen

Read the best books first, or you may not have a chance to read them at all – Henry David Thoreau

It has been said that books find their own readers – but sometimes they need someone to show them the way – Carsten Henn

Contents

Introduction

Read the World aims to inspire readers to get to know the world better by recommending the best three books on more than 50 countries in Africa, the Middle East, Asia and Latin America. The mix of nonfiction and novels – both classic and contemporary – goes beyond books merely set on location, looking instead to those that capture a nation's spirit and reveal something of its soul. Of the three books listed for each country, generally two are fiction – often historical or state-of-the-nation novels giving voice to native authors – and the third is nonfiction. As the US author EL Doctorow said: "The historian will tell you what happened. The novelist will tell you what it felt like."

This book started out as a feature in the Guardian, and has been extensively revised and expanded. It offers a literary tour of the global south, encouraging readers to journey into new areas and experiences, encountering different peoples and places. And what could be better than to be guided by smart, erudite and often eminent novelists, historians and journalists.

With independence a seminal event for many global south nations in the 20th century, several novels listed reflect the anti-colonial struggle. The Nigerian writer China Achebe said that "until the lions have their own historians, the history of the hunt will always glorify the hunter". As the literary lions roar, they not only tell us about their own countries, but also about the former colonial masters. Salman Rushdie called it "the empire writes back".

There are further recommendations of works by the authors mentioned, and also "Read on" suggestions in each country for those who want to extend their journey. The books are arranged geographically by continent and then alphabetically by country.

I hope intrepid travellers who wish to experience a country rather than just visit it and armchair adventurers who want to globetrot while sitting at home will appreciate Read the World. The books chosen are intended to open windows to other worlds and to see the world through other people's eyes, breaking down barriers and bounding across borders. In doing so, they can deepen our understanding of different peoples and cultures, and help to reduce the distance between them and us. Books can change lives, and the power of the pen (or keyboard) is not to be underestimated.

So whether spurred by wonder or wanderlust, cross continents and cultures as you read your way across the globe – from Mexico City to Manila or Buenos Aires to Beijing, via the Middle East and Africa. Read the World is both a road map and a reader's ticket to great literature. Enjoy the journey!

Africa

Angola

Rainy Season by José Eduardo Agualusa (1996), translated by Daniel Hahn

Agualusa's novel, ostensibly about the life of the Angolan poet and activist Lidía do Carmo Ferreira – who mysteriously vanished in the capital Luanda in 1992 – depicts his country's tortured history in the second half of the 20th century. Angola's independence in 1975, after a long anti-colonial struggle against Portugal, brings cause for celebration but also marks the beginning of three decades of unrelenting civil war.

Agualusa entwines fact and fiction to introduce various characters whose lives interconnect, and the story flits between colonial times, the civil-war era and the present. He never loses control of his tangled web of a tale, told mostly by a journalist investigating the disappearance of Carmo Ferreira.

Following independence, rivalry between the anti-colonial groups and factionalism within the ruling People's Movement for the Liberation of Angola (MPLA) spiral into chaos and violence. Intellectuals and artists are caught up in the internecine struggle, which devastates the country and brings new horrors as rebels and dissidents are jailed, tortured and killed. The urgent, lyrical prose brings home the torment and disillusionment as the Angolan revolution feeds on its protagonists and destroys their idealism. Anguished and sometimes harrowing, its intellectual and emotional drive makes Rainy Season hard to put down.

Angolan-born journalist and writer Agualusa lives between Angola, his country of birth, Portugal and Brazil.
See also: A General Theory of Oblivion (2012); The Book of Chameleons (2004), both translated by Daniel Hahn

The Return of the Water Spirit by Pepetela (1995), translated by Luís R Mitras

Pepetela's political fable is a stinging critique of corruption in post-colonial Angola. It's set during the late 1980s and early 1990s as the socialist MPLA government embraces capitalism and the disgruntled Unita opposition rekindles the civil war.

Carmina Evangelista, an energetic and ambitious ruling party member – and once-fanatical leftwinger – switches seamlessly from Marx to market forces, and makes a fortune supplying arms to the government. Her lazy, obsequious husband João, consumed with playing computer games, rarely bothers to turn up for work as a government employee.

Meanwhile, the buildings in the capital's central Kinaxixi Square are mysteriously crumbling – a phenomenon dubbed "Luanda Syndrome" – baffling engineers and scientists. What's causing it? Is it God's punishment of a degenerate society, sabotage by the Americans, or the water spirit, Kianda, reclaiming the land for the lagoon that it once was? Amid all the confusion and cynicism, the only glimmer of hope comes from the grassroots "naked movement", led by those left with nothing after their homes are reduced to rubble. The novel offers a short, sharp satire on a decaying country whose people have been betrayed by their leaders.

Pepetela is the guerrilla alias and pen name of former MPLA combatant and one-time deputy minister Artur Carlos Maurício Pestana.

See also: Mayombe (1979), translated by Michael Wolfers

Blue Dahlia, Black Gold by Daniel Metcalfe (2013)

Welcome to Angola ... a petrostate of plenty amid grinding poverty, where beer costs less than bottled water and the oil-soaked rich are buying up chunks of Portugal, home of the former colonisers. Metcalfe, an intrepid traveller in this "anti-tourist destination", has an insatiable curiosity and a determination to get under the skin of this complex and contradictory country. Weaving history and politics into his travelogue, he tells of the Portuguese colonial era, the crippling 27-year, post-independence Angolan civil war, and the ruling MPLA party's iron grip on the state.

He notes that an oil boom brought the country extraordinary wealth, but failed to benefit the vast majority of Angolans as the MPLA eschewed Marxism for a cocktail of capitalism, cronyism and corruption.

Metcalfe embarks on bone-jarring journeys across the country – talking to activists, expat landmine clearers, tribal elders and citizens – unfailingly mining interesting stories. Despite facing something rotten in the state of Angola, there is no doubting people's resilience. One woman who helps Metcalfe tackle the country's ubiquitous red tape has "something quietly courageous about her ... like a delicate bird in a cage, she found a way to sing".

The British journalist's subtle wit and sharp eye are the hallmarks of this enriching and enjoyable introduction to an African powerhouse.

See also: Out of Steppe (1999)

Read on

Good Morning Comrades by Ondjaki (2001), translated by Stephen Henighan; Magnificent and Beggar Land: Angola Since the Civil War by Ricardo Soares de Oliveira (2014); Another Day of Life by Ryszard Kapuscinski (1976), translated by William Brand and Katarzyna Mroczkowska-Brand; In the Name of the People: Angola's Forgotten Massacre by Lara Pawson (2014); Our Musseque by Jose Luandino Vieira (2003), translated by Robin Patterson

Democratic Republic of the Congo

The Poisonwood Bible by Barbara Kingsolver (1998)

Kingsolver's riveting doorstopper (weighing in at more than 600 pages) is set in 1959, just a year before the country gains its independence from Belgium. It tells the story of an American Baptist missionary, Nathan Price, who drags his wife and four daughters from the US state of Georgia to a remote village in Congo to deliver the message of his god to the natives.

The Poisonwood Bible spans 30 years in the life of the family as it slowly implodes – under pressures brought on by the bloody-minded father/preacher as well as political and social upheaval within the country – and then rebuilds itself. Congo pervades the story, as the country grapples with its fledgling independence and a descent into violence exacerbated by the machinations of the colonial power and the CIA.

The polyphonic novel is written from the perspectives of the missionary's wife, Orleanna Price, and her daughters, who each tell the story in turn. We never hear directly from Nathan, but his presence and stifling righteousness loom large, and the King James Bible echoes through the storytelling. Kingsolver passionately plays out her politics as she skewers colonialism, patriarchy and religious fanaticism, while also reflecting on guilt and personal responsibility.

The American author, who lived briefly in the Congo as a child, says she "spent nearly 30 years waiting for the wisdom and maturity to write this book". The result is hugely ambitious and immensely enjoyable.

See also: Demon Copperhead (2022); The Lacuna (2009)

Before the Birth of the Moon by Valentin Y Mudimbe (1976), translated by Marjolijn de Jager

Set in the 1960s, shortly after Congo's independence, Mudimbe's story reflects the political uncertainty and instability of the period. It's told through the complex relationship between a government minister (known only as The Minister) and a prostitute named Ya, who meet in the steamy world of Kinshasa's bars and nightclubs.

The Minister is attracted by the wealth and power of office, and appears to have little concern for his country or its people. Ya left her village to avoid an arranged marriage, and has her heart set on enjoying life in the big city. She wants nothing to do with the anti-government rebellion of her tribe, which is led by her father, a village chief.

Loyalty, deceit and greed lie at the heart of the tale, and each protagonist has committed a grievous act of betrayal against the other, which costs them dear. Their personal stories are inextricably linked to the turmoil within the country as it struggles for nationhood, and neither The Minister nor Ya can escape the tumultuous events taking place.

Mudimbe, a respected philosopher and writer on Africa, was born in what was then the Belgian Congo. He teaches literature at Duke University in the US.

See also: The Invention of Africa: Gnosis, Philosophy and the Order of Knowledge (1988)

Dancing in the Glory of Monsters by Jason Stearns (2011)

Stearns details how after the 1994 genocide in Rwanda the conflict between Tutsis and Hutus spilled over into neighbouring Congo, unleashing a tangled web of wars. Fuelled by ethnic rivalries and hunger for the country's rich mineral deposits, "Africa's world war" – fought in a country the size of western Europe – sucked in the armies of nine nations, along with a bewildering range of militias.

More than 5 million people have died, and hundreds of thousands of women have been raped. The world mostly looked away, perhaps because this "endless war" became ever more messy and complex. Stearns bravely sets out to counter the west's indifference and ignorance, doing much dangerous and arduous legwork to hear from key players – both perpetrators and victims – and eyewitnesses. He attempts to understand why Congo has been in turmoil for decades and stability has been so elusive.

The account of this brutal and labyrinthine conflict is not for the faint-hearted. But although it's a complicated tale with no heroes or happy endings, it's still gripping – delivered with empathy, and backed up by meticulous fact-finding.

Stearns, an American human rights activist, has lived and worked in Congo and been an intrepid observer of the country for more than a decade.

See also: The War That Doesn't Say Its Name: The Unending Conflict in the Congo (2022)

Read on

King Leopold's Ghost: A Story of Greed, Terror and Heroism in Colonial Africa by Adam Hochschild (1998); Congo: The Epic History of a People by David Van Reybrouck (2010), translated by Sam Garrett; Cobalt Red: How the Blood of the Congo Powers Our Lives by Siddarth Kara (2022); Tram 83 by Fiston Mwanza Mujila (2015), translated by Roland Glasser; The Assassination of Lumumba by Ludo De Witte (1999), translated by Ann Wright and Renée Fenby; The Rebels' Hour by Lieve Joris (2006), translated by Liz Waters

Ethiopia

Cutting for Stone by Abraham Verghese (2009)

In 1954, a young Indian nun working at a mission hospital in Addis Ababa dies while giving birth to identical twins. Their father, a well-respected British surgeon, disappears, abandoning the boys. Fortunately for the twins, the two doctors who deliver them become their loving, adoptive parents.

This big, bittersweet, beautifully written novel, set mostly around the hospital, follows the family's fortunes over five decades. As the boys come of age, Ethiopia's turbulent politics – executions, rebellions, coups – play out sometimes on the periphery of their personal story and sometimes at its very centre.

The "elder" twin, Marion, narrates the tale, at the heart of which is a betrayal that breaks the strong bond between him and his brother Shiva. When political events take a dangerous turn, forcing Marion to flee to New York, he finds himself becoming entangled with his past and forced to come to terms with it.

Verghese, an acute observer, vividly evokes life at the hospital and in the bustling Ethiopian capital. He delivers a page-turning, emotionally absorbing tale – despite a surfeit of medical detail (the book's title is a phrase from the Hippocratic oath). The Ethiopian-born author is a doctor who lives, writes and teaches medicine in the US. This, his first novel, has sold more than a million copies.

See also: The Covenant of Water (2023)

Beneath the Lion's Gaze by Maaza Mengiste (2011)

Mengiste's novel of the early years of Ethiopia's revolution begins in 1974 as student demonstrations and famine lead to the overthrow of Emperor Haile Selassie by the military. She creates an intimate portrait of an extended family, and it is through their eyes that we see the revolution unfolding – and descending into chaos and callousness.

Hailu, a respected surgeon in Addis Ababa, and his elder son Yonas, a university professor, prefer to keep their distance from Ethiopia's violent and dangerous politics. But the younger son, Dawit, is determined to be politically active. Initially, he is a student protester against the emperor and supports the

Marxist junta. Later, when the military begins to crush dissent and sow terror, he becomes a brave and dogged opponent of the regime. Dawit recalls his mother telling him that "hope can never come from doing nothing".

When the military forces Hailu to treat a young woman who has been horrifically tortured, a decision he makes causes him and his family to be swept up in the political storm. This compassionate, tightly woven tale immediately draws the reader into its unfurling domestic and political drama. It's an impressive literary debut.

Mengiste's family left Ethiopia when she was a child, and she now lives in the US.

See also: The Shadow King (2019)

Notes From the Hyena's Belly by Nega Mezlekia (2000)

Mezlekia's poignant memoir recounts his coming of age in the turbulent decades straddling the ousting of Haile Selassie. Born in Jijiga, a city where Amhara Christians and ethnic Somali Muslims live in "a multicultural mixing bowl", he has fond recollections of family life and early schooldays. However, the best of times in childhood is followed by the worst of times in adolescence as Ethiopia endures famine, civil war, repression and war with neighbouring Somalia.

As his political awareness grows, Mezlekia joins student protests calling for land reform. But the struggle is to be "long and treacherous". His first spell in prison, where torture is routine, is at the age of 14 – followed by many more. In 1977-78, the Marxist military rulers unleash their Red Terror, leaving 100,000 young people dead in the carnage. With "the revolution eating Ethiopia's children at an alarming rate", Mezlekia, aged 18, joins an armed rebel group. But ethnic tensions within the group eventually force him to leave, and he slips back into civilian life.

Despite the harsh realities, Mezlekia tells his story – and the story of his country – with wry humour, interspersing facts with folktales. It's an insider's insight into contemporary Ethiopia. Both his father and his beloved Mam meet violent deaths. Miraculously Mezlekia survives, leaving Ethiopia for Europe and then Canada, where he lives today.

See also: ub (2001); The Unfortunate Marriage of Azeb Yitades (2006)

Read on

The Abiy Project: God, Power and War in the New Ethiopia by Tom Gardener (2024); The Wife's Tale by Aida Edemariam (2018); Oromay by Baalu Girma (1983), translated by David DeGusta and Mesfin Felleke Yirgu; The Emperor: Downfall of an Autocrat by Ryszard Kapuscinski (1978), translated by William R Brand and Katarzyna Mroczkowska-Brand; The Chains of Heaven: An Ethiopian Romance by Philip Marsden (2005); A History of Ethiopia by Harold G Marcus (1994/2002); Yohannes Ishi by Nabse Bamato (2014)

Ghana

The Beautyful Ones Are Not Yet Born by Ayi Kwei Armah (1968)

A railway clerk in Accra, who is the unnamed narrator of this morality tale, strives to maintain his integrity amid the corruption that surrounds him in newly independent Ghana. His refusal to accept bribes, despite struggling to make ends meet on his meagre salary, angers those around him – especially his acquisitive wife. They can't understand why he won't do what everyone else is doing.

The high hopes he had for the country at independence have soured, and he is bitter that things have grown rotten "with such obscene haste". "The man", as the narrator is referred to, views the new leaders as trying "to be the dark ghosts of Europeans", aping the repression and rapacity of the country's former white colonial masters.

Armah's acerbic debut novel excoriates President Kwame Nkrumah's government for the graft and extortion that were rife in 1960s Ghana. A military coup in 1966 overthrows Nkrumah but, rather than heralding better days to come, it merely brings "another group of bellies [that] will be bursting with the country's riches".

As the man continues to grapple with providing for his wife and children and resisting "the rot" he sees everywhere, a misspelled inscription on a bus (which provides the book's title) offers a sliver of hope for an end to the ugly realities of the day.

Armah, who was born in the Gold Coast (now Ghana), lives as something of a recluse in Dakar, Senegal.

See also: Two Thousand Seasons (1973); Fragments (1970)

Changes: A Love Story by Ama Ata Aidoo (1991)

Aidoo's provocative and engaging tale of a young woman in modern-day Accra who challenges sexism and social mores resonates beyond Ghana. Esi Sekyi, a smart, spirited career woman, feels stifled in her marriage. Finding her ambitions curbed and freedoms constrained by her husband, she decides to divorce him.

No one Esi knows is remotely sympathetic. Her sharp-tongued grandmother chastises her, saying women must do "the serious business of living with our heads and never our hearts". And her best friend, Opokuya Dakwa, who wants more freedom in her own marriage, reminds her: "Our people have said that for any marriage to work, one party has to be a fool ... And they really mean the woman."

Esi meets Ali Kondey, a successful businessman, and is charmed by him. They become lovers, and Ali – a Muslim who is married and has children – urges Esi to become his second wife. Curiously for such a fiercely independent woman, she agrees. Later, as disillusionment with her polygamous marriage sets in, she reflects on life "stretching ahead like the Yendi-Tamale road when it was first constructed: straight, flat and endless".

Aidoo wears her feminism on her sleeve, and gets her message across with sly humour. The author, who died in 2023, was also a poet and playwright, and served briefly as minister of education in the 1980s.

See also: No Sweetness Here and Other Stories (1969); The Girl Who Can and Other Stories (1997)

My First Coup D'etat by John Dramani Mahama (2012)

Mahama's first coup – which he experienced as a seven-year-old – was the army's 1966 ousting of Nkrumah, who had led Ghana to independence from Britain nine years earlier. It proved to be a life-changing experience for the author. His father, a government minister, was held by the military for more than a year and came back a changed man.

Reinventing himself as a rice farmer, Mahama Sr became extremely wealthy. He eventually returned to politics, only to be forced to flee the country after yet another coup. His father plays a big part in Mahama's endearing memoir, in which the author recounts his coming of age – in tandem with his newly independent country – during Africa's "lost decades". During that bleak post-colonial period, from the late 60s to the 90s, the continent was bedevilled by economic stagnation and political turbulence.

Mahama delivers an intimate, insider's account through personal stories, and weaves in some of Ghana's own progress and pitfalls along the way. The cycle of coups finally ended in 1992, when the country adopted a new constitution and entered into an era of democracy that brought "the return of hope".

Like his father, Mahama went into politics. He published this book during his term as vice-president, and went on to serve as president from 2012 to 2017. He was re-elected as president in 2024.

Read on

Homegoing by Yaa Gyasi (2016); The Ghana Reader: History, Culture, Politics, edited by Kwasi Konadu and Clifford C Campbell (2016); Hold by Michael Donkor (2018); The Hundred Wells of Salaga by Ayesha Harruna Attah (2018); Tail of the Blue Bird by Nii Ayikwei Parkes (2009); Hurricane of Dust by Amy Djoleto (1987)

Kenya

A Grain of Wheat by Ngũgĩ wa Thiong'o (1967)

On the threshold of independence in 1963, the residents of Thabai village prepare to celebrate the ceding of power to Kenyans. But beneath the surface, tension is simmering: the British colonisers are finally leaving and the native Kenyans have scores to settle.

During the struggle for independence, some villagers signed up with the Home Guard and collaborated with the "white man". Others took the Mau Mau oath and joined the rebellion, and were imprisoned and tortured in British internment camps. The comrades of Kihika, a local rebel leader who was captured and hanged, are determined to find and kill the man who betrayed him.

The stories of the main characters are told through cleverly winding back and forth between past and present. The political turbulence in the country deeply affected people's lives, testing their friendships, love and courage – and sometimes led to betrayal. As this compelling tale unfolds, each chapter fills in pieces of a puzzle. Ngũgĩ creates a vivid history of the independence struggle, retelling the colonial story from a Kenyan viewpoint.

Kenya's most famous novelist spent more than a year in prison for his writings during the 1970s, and later went into exile abroad. He lives in the US.

See also: Petals of Blood (1977); Weep Not Child (1964); The River Between (1965)

Coming to Birth by Marjorie Oludhe Macgoye (1986)

The titular coming to birth involves Paulina Were's transition from bewildered 16-year-old bride to self-confident, independent woman. And as a backdrop there's the coming to birth of Kenya, from British colonial rule to independence and fragile democracy.

Paulina leaves her small village to join Martin, her new husband, in big, bustling Nairobi, arriving as a frightened, friendless woman in a city under martial law. As she begins to find her feet, Martin's attempts to curb her new-found freedoms sours their relationship. Their marriage troubled and childless, the couple eventually drift apart and Paulina returns to her village.

There, she finds work as a teacher and seamstress, and increasingly lives apart from her husband – no easy task in Kenya's male-dominated society. Martin has several casual "city wives" and Paulina has a child by another man. But the bond between them is never fully broken.

Macgoye's pithy tale allows us to see the making of modern Kenya through the eyes of an ordinary, quietly determined woman as she makes her way – as does her country – through often turbulent social and political change.

The British-born author went to Kenya in 1954 as a missionary and bookseller, and lived there until her death in 2015. As well as a novelist, she was a poet and a social activist.
See also: Victoria and Murder in Majengo (1993)

It's Our Turn to Eat by Michela Wrong (2009)

Wrong's book on the rise and fall of Kenya's anti-corruption tsar reads in parts like a Le Carré-style political thriller – and points to massive moral failure. At its heart is the practice of competing ethnic elites taking turns at grabbing power and "eating" – which is what Kenyans call the gorging on state resources by the well-connected.

John Githongo, a bright, idealistic young Kenyan, is appointed by the government to root out sleaze. But within two years he

has to flee the country in fear for his life after discovering that the administration and its friends are brazenly looting public funds. Githongo, who turns up at Wrong's flat in London, blows the whistle, backing up his allegations with secretly taped conversations. But it changes little – even western agencies are complicit, with most donors turning a blind eye to the revelations.

The book ends just after the horrific ethnic violence surrounding the 2007 elections, which Wrong argues was caused by the country's tribal-based, winner-takes-all politics. When local shops refused to stock It's Our Turn to Eat because of Kenya's draconian libel laws, it briefly became the most pirated text in the country's history.

British author and journalist Wrong has reported from across Africa for many years, and has written books on the Democratic Republic of the Congo, Eritrea and Rwanda.

See also: Do Not Disturb: The Story of a Political Murder and an African Regime Gone Bad (2021); I Didn't Do It For You: How the World Used and Abused a Small African Nation (2005)

Read on

Dust by Yvonne Adhiambo Owuor (2013); One Day I Will Write About This Place by Binyavanga Wainaina (2011); Trapped in History: Kenya, Mau Mau and Me by Nicholas Rankin (2023); The In-Between World of Vikram Lall by MG Vassanji (2003); Going Down River Road by Meja Mwangi (1976); The River and the

Source by Margaret A Ogola (1994); Who Will Catch Us As We Fall by Iman Verjee (2016)

Mozambique

Sleepwalking Land by Mia Couto (1992), translated by David Brookshaw

During Mozambique's long, vicious civil war in the 1980s, an old man and an orphaned boy fleeing the conflict take refuge in a burnt-out bus strewn with corpses. Beside one of the bodies the boy finds a diary, from which he begins to read to his elderly companion. It tells the story – laced with magic realism – of Kindzu, a young man who seeks to play a more honourable role in the war by searching out and joining a mystical band of warriors called naparamas. The elusive naparamas fight against the murderous militias and bandits ravaging the land.

In the desolate landscape the boy and the old man venture out daily to forage for food, careful to avoid marauding combatants. As the days go by, they are increasingly caught up with Kindzu's tale which, as it progresses, becomes seamlessly entangled with their own story.

Couto's beautifully written, angry novel examines the devastation wrought by the conflict in post-colonial Mozambique, ultimately delivering a searing indictment of war – which, in a memorable turn of phrase, he calls "a snake that bites us with our own teeth".

The author, born in Mozambique to Portuguese exiles, is a journalist, poet, novelist and environmental biologist. An international panel at the 2002 Zimbabwe book fair chose this, his first novel, as one of the 12 best African books of the 20th century. *See also: Under the Frangipani (1996); The Last Flight of the Flamingo (2000), both translated by David Brookshaw; Sea Loves Me: Selected Stories (2021), translated by David Brookshaw and Eric MB Becker*

The First Wife: A Tale of Polygamy by Paulina Chiziane (2002), translated by David Brookshaw

Having been married to Tony, a Maputo police chief, for 20 years, his wife Rami discovers that her husband is a serial philanderer with a string of mistresses (four, to be exact) and an array of children.

After Rami's initial shock, and violent confrontations with some of her rival lovers, she and the other women decide to band together and fight back. The women, with their 21 children in tow, ambush Tony at his 50th birthday party, forcing him to marry them all under polygamy rules, pay their bride prices and adhere to a strict conjugal rota. But life can interfere with the best-laid plans – and one event in particular changes everything.

The story is narrated by Rami, the "first wife", who sees polygamy as feeding a man's vanity. For a woman, it means "to have a man in your arms while he yearns for another … Loving a polygamist is to chew pain by way of nourishment, to fill your belly by swallowing your saliva."

This furious satire makes some scalpel-sharp observations on its way to skewering a misogynistic society in which women are beaten down by tradition and a colonial mindset. Although set in Mozambique, it reveals some universal and ugly truths about living under an unreconstructed patriarchy.

Chiziane, the first Mozambican woman to publish a novel, prefers to call herself a storyteller rather than a writer.

See also: The Joyful Song of the Partridge (2024), translated by David Brookshaw

Go Tell the Crocodiles: Chasing Prosperity in Mozambique by Rowan Moore Gerety (2018)

"The subject of peace in Mozambique is very sensitive," the former archbishop of Beira city tells Gerety. Jaime Pedro Gonçalves was a leading light in the talks that, in 1992, ended the 16-year post-independence civil war. It had claimed a million lives. Two decades later the war came close to erupting again, threatening to exacerbate the country's economic crisis and overwhelm its fragile democracy.

The former archbishop is one of the people through whose life Gerety provides colourful and enlightening snapshots of contemporary Mozambique. Among the others are the opposition leader Afonso Dhlakama (who died in 2018), a poor farmer, a street seller and a former mercenary.

The west's focus on getting the Marxist Frelimo to embrace capitalism, rather than on nurturing democracy and tackling corruption, has allowed the ruling party to establish something akin to a one-party state since independence from Portugal in 1975. The winner-takes-all politics has bred a kleptocratic elite; the opposition was led by an ageing warlord who used violence as a political tool; land disputes threaten to oust farmers from their holdings; and people on the margins struggle to make ends meet.

Despite all that, the country is touted as an African success story because of its once rapid economic growth. It appears that although Mozambicans are chasing prosperity, few outside a small political elite actually catch up with it.

Gerety, a Miami-based journalist, was a Fulbright scholar in Mozambique.

Read on

A Short History of Mozambique by Malyn Newitt (2017); Neighbours: The Story of a Murder by Lilia Momple (2001), translated by Richard Bartlett and Isaura de Oliveira; Ualalapi by Ungulani Ba Ka Khosa (1987), translated by Richard Bartlett and Isaura de Oliveira; We Killed Mangy-Dog and Other Mozambique Stories by Luis Bernardo Honwana (1964), translated by Dorothy Guedes

Nigeria

Things Fall Apart by Chinua Achebe (1958)

Achebe is regarded as the father (perhaps now grandfather) of modern African literature. His first novel – a riposte to what he saw as misrepresentations and distortions in Joseph Conrad's Heart of Darkness – has become a classic, and is one of the most widely read African novels. Set during the scramble for Africa by the European powers in the 1890s, Things Fall Apart portrays the devastating impact of English Christian missionaries and colonial laws on Igbo culture.

The novel tells the tragic story of Okonkwo, a powerful and ambitious warrior among Nigeria's Igbo people who is forced into a seven-year exile for accidentally killing a member of his clan. When he returns, he finds that traditional life is being corroded by the encroaching colonisers. When he and others who are unwilling to adapt try to combat this outside influence, things fall apart.

Achebe is a sympathetic voice, but he refuses to romanticise pre-colonial life and pulls no punches in revealing the flaws of his characters. Through this novel, for the first time, outsiders were able to see Africans as they saw themselves.

Achebe was a constant thorn in the side of Nigerian military governments over the years, and that often meant going into exile. The novelist, who died in 2013, was also a poet and an academic.

See also: Arrow of God (1964); Anthills of Savannah (1987); A Man of the People (1966)

Half of a Yellow Sun by Chimamanda Ngozi Adichie (2006)

Adichie's magnificently eloquent novel spans the decade to the end of the 1967-70 secessionist Biafran war, which tore Nigeria apart and claimed millions of lives. The intelligent, compassionate story intertwines the lives and different worlds of five protagonists, among them a charismatic, revolutionary academic, his beautiful partner and their houseboy, who develops a fierce loyalty to his employers.

As the conflict deepens, the Igbo population in the war-affected region suffer as they are sucked into hunger, squalor and violence. Personal and private struggles take centre stage as friendships and loyalties are severely tested, but the story encompasses wider themes such as post-colonialism, ethnic loyalties and race.

Adichie perfectly captures the period's pain and poignancy as the new nation's hopes and dreams – represented by the half of a yellow sun emblem that appears on Biafra's flag – flower briefly, before being crushed. One of the characters in the novel is writing a book titled The World Was Silent When We Died. As if in response, Half of a Yellow Sun provides a cogent history lesson that brings a distant war up close and works as a powerful antidote to forgetting.

Born after the war, the author grew up "in the shadow of Biafra" in the university town of Nsukka, which features in the book.

See also: Purple Hibiscus (2003); Americanah (2013); Dream Count (2025)

A Swamp Full of Dollars: Pipelines and Paramilitaries at Nigeria's Oil Frontier by Michael Peel (2009)

In Nigeria, oil is a dirty business. The black gold of the Niger delta pollutes the region's air, land and water, and the corruption it generates poisons the country's business and politics.

The crude oil from sub-Saharan Africa's largest producer also stains western society – which is hooked on oil – and its financial institutions, into which much ill-gotten gain from Nigeria flows. "[It is] hard to imagine a dirtier business in which so many of us in the rich world are so intimately involved," writes Peel, outlining how Britain and the US profit greatly from the kleptocracy created by Nigeria's elite. Meanwhile, anger in the oil-rich delta, where people feel cheated out of their share of the profits, has sparked a violent response. Peel fearlessly ventures into the militants' swamp hideouts in the lawless region – "a trouble spot as hot as the local pepper soup" – where millions of dollars of oil have been siphoned off to fuel the insurgency.

In his lively prose and sharp analysis revealing the horrors wrought by "the curse of oil in Africa", Peel's scorn for the authorities responsible for this sorry state of affairs is matched by a genuine affection for the country and its inhabitants. The author, a Financial Times journalist, was formerly the paper's west Africa correspondent, based in Lagos.

Read on

Chronicles From the Land of the Happiest People on Earth by Wole Soyinka (2021); Stay with Me by Ayobami Adebayo (2017); The Girl With the Louding Voice by Abi Daré (2020); Looking for Transwonderland: Travels in Nigeria by Noo Saro-Wiwa (2012); Welcome to Lagos by Chibundu Onuzo (2017); The Famished Road by Ben Okri (1991); The Road to the Country by Chigozie Obioma (2024); Nearly All the Men in Lagos Are Mad by Dami-lare Kuku (2021); The Secret Lives of Baba Segi's Wives by Lola Shoneyin (2010)

Rwanda

We Wish to Inform You That Tomorrow We Will Be Killed With Our Families: Stories From Rwanda by Philip Gourevitch (1998)

In 1994 Rwanda's extremist government, under attack by an invading rebel army, urged the country's Hutu majority to annihilate its Tutsi minority. Over 100 days, more than 800,000 Rwandans – the vast majority Tutsis – were hacked to death by Hutus, often their neighbours, friends, even family.

Gourevitch offers a powerful and chilling chronicle of the genocide and its aftermath. The title comes from a note written by Tutsi pastors of a church – sheltering terrified Tutsi men, women and children – to the leader of their religious order, a Hutu, but it was ignored. The mass slaughter only ended when the Tutsi rebel army, the Rwandan Patriotic Front, which had invaded from neighbouring Uganda four years earlier, ousted the government. However, conflict and killings persisted as Hutus fled to refugee camps controlled by extremists in neighbouring Zaire (now Congo) and were pursued by the RPF.

The international community is excoriated for its inaction during the genocide: although UN troops were present in Rwanda, they failed to intervene as the killings raged.

The book examines the historical context that led to the tragedy, including the role of the Belgian colonial power in fomenting and exacerbating ethnic divisions. The author speaks to survivors, perpetrators, witnesses and military men to untangle what happened. He doesn't shy away from the gut-wrenching savagery of the events, and his research and reportage are delivered through propulsive storytelling.

Gourevitch is a longtime contributor to the New Yorker magazine.

See also: The Ballad of Abu Ghraib by Philip Gourevitch and Errol Morris (2008)

Our Lady of the Nile by Scholastique Mukasonga (2012), translated by Melanie Mauthner

Mukasonga's acclaimed debut novel is set in an exclusive girls' boarding school run by Belgian nuns high in Rwanda's mountains, near the source of the Nile. It's a coming-of-age tale in which a group of young women learn about identity and belonging.

The daughters of the elite are sent to the school to shield them from the violence brewing outside. But as friendships are formed and rivalries fester, the simmering tensions at the school reflect the country's ethnic antagonism in the late 1970s, presaging the 1994 genocide. Despite Rwanda's independence, a colonial mentality persists at the school: the girls must use Christian names rather than their Rwandan ones, they must speak only in French, and the curriculum glorifies Europe and belittles Africa.

Veronica and her friend Virginia, who have been admitted under a strict 10% quota for Tutsis, come up against the dorm bully, Gloriosa. The daughter of a senior Hutu politician, Gloriosa has imbibed all her parents' prejudices and seeks to eradicate the country's Tutsi "cockroaches". Amid prejudice and persecution, deceit and danger, the story carries a growing sense of menace. When Gloriosa lies about being attacked by Tutsi thugs outside the school, events spiral out of control.

Mukasonga's writing is both lyrical and evocative as her tale builds steadily to its denouement. The Rwandan-born author, who moved to France in 1992, lost more than 30 members of her family in the 1994 killings.

See also: Cockroaches, translated by Jordan Stump (2016); Kibogo, translated by Mark Polizzotti (2023)

Do Not Disturb: The Story of a Political Murder and an African Regime Gone Bad by Michela Wrong (2021)

Is President Paul Kagame a hero who ended the genocide against the Tutsis and put Rwanda on the road to peace and prosperity? Or is he a ruthless dictator whose regime brooks no dissent and murders its critics?

Wrong endorses the latter view. Her detailed and devastating critique of the regime focuses on the aftermath of the 1994 genocide. It challenges the ruling Tutsi-dominated RPF's carefully curated narrative of bridging the ethnic divide and delivering economic success, and accuses Kagame of suppressing political opposition – with dissidents facing exile and assassination.

"Do not disturb" was the sign Patrick's Karegeya's killers hung on the door of his hotel room in South Africa after murdering him in 2014. The former Rwandan intelligence chief had had a high-profile falling out with Kagame, his erstwhile schoolmate and close comrade. Kagame denied complicity in the murder but added, chillingly: "I wish Rwanda had done it." The book's narrative is woven around Karegeya's story.

The Rwandan army, meanwhile, is accused of gross human rights violations in neighbouring Democratic Republic of the Congo (DRC), where up to 2 million Hutus fled after the genocide, and of pillaging its diamonds and minerals to finance the Kigali regime.

Wrong alleges that a guilt-ridden west – which failed to halt the genocide – has turned a blind eye to Kagame's abuses, adopting him as its favourite dictator and showering Rwanda with aid.

The British author and journalist has written books on the DRC, Kenya and Eritrea.

See also: It's Our Turn to Eat (2009); I Didn't Do It For You: How the World Used and Abused a Small African Nation (2005)

Read on

Small Country by Gaël Faye (2016), translated by Sarah Ardizzone; All Your Children, Scattered by Beata Umubyeyi Mairesse (2022), translated by Alison Anderson; Running the Rift by Naomi Benaron (2010); Bad News: Last Journalists in a Dictatorship by Anjan Sundaram (2016); A Sunday At The Pool In Kigali by Gil Courtemanche (2000), translated by Patricia Claxton; Murambi, The Book of Bones by Boubacar Boris Diop (2000), translated by Fiona McLaughlin

Senegal

God's Bits of Wood by Ousmane Sembène (1960), translated by Francis Price

Sembène's stirring tale of the 1947-48 Dakar-Niger railway strike in French colonial west Africa is based on actual events in which he participated. The struggle for better wages and conditions takes place in Dakar, Thiès and Bamako, and the story – with its large cast of characters – travels back and forth between the cities.

The workers are bullied, beaten and even killed as the French try to break the strike. Later, the authorities attempt to starve the strikers into submission by cutting off supplies of food and water. Although the striking workers are male, women play a pivotal role, gaining in confidence and status as they forage for food, militantly support the strikers, and confront the colonial troops sent to suppress the strike.

Sembène's indictment of colonialism exposes the racism, oppression and poverty endured by the workers and their families. One matriarch involved in the strike says: "Real misfortune is not just a matter of being hungry and thirsty; it is a matter of knowing that there are people who want you to be hungry and thirsty."

This memorable novel was published in 1960, the year Senegal became independent. Sembène (1923-2007), born in Senegal's Casamance region, was a fisherman, soldier, dock worker in France and union organiser before becoming a writer – and then a seminal film-maker, considered the father of African film. *See also: Xala (1973); The Money Order With White Genesis (1965), both translated by Clive Wake*

So Long a Letter by Mariama Bâ (1979), translated by Modupé Bodé-Thomas

Bâ's debut novella takes the form of a letter from a recently widowed Muslim schoolteacher, Ramatoulaye, to her best friend Aissatou. Writing after the death of her estranged husband, Ramatoulaye, in her long and moving missive, unveils the stories of the two women. Both are pushing back against the constraints imposed on them by a conservative Muslim community.

Ramatoulaye feels her husband humiliated and betrayed her when – after 30 years of marriage and 12 children – he took their teenage daughter's school friend as his second wife under Islamic tenets and abandoned his first wife. "He burned his past," she says, "both morally and materially."

Although Aissatou divorced her husband when he took a second wife, Ramatoulaye refused to do so. "Even though I respect the choice of liberated women," she writes, "I have never conceived of happiness outside marriage." Little by little, she reveals a quiet strength as she becomes more independent, battling to survive as a single mother in a changing, post-colonial society where the odds are still stacked against women.

Despite her struggles, she remains optimistic, saying "hope still lives on within me".

Bâ's conversational prose exudes an enchanting intimacy and warmth, and So Long a Letter is considered a classic of African feminist fiction. Dakar-born Bâ, a former schoolteacher, died aged 52 in 1981 after a long illness.

See also: The Scarlet Song (1981), translated by Dorothy S Blair

Fishermen's Blues: A West African Community at Sea by Anna Badkhen (2018)

Badkhen beautifully captures the rhythms of daily life in Joal, Senegal's largest artisanal fishing port and birthplace of the country's favourite son and first president, Léopold Senghor. Fishermen's boats have set out to sea from the port for hundreds of years – artisanal fishing is the country's main resource and biggest earner of foreign exchange. However, the once-abundant fish stocks are now but a memory as the community faces the perils of overfishing and climate change, which have decimated harvests.

"The sea is broken," the fishermen say. "The sea is empty. The genies have taken the fish elsewhere." They employ techniques both old and new – mixing superstition with skill, and genies with GPSs – as they are forced to undertake longer and more dangerous journeys chasing catches off the Gambia or down the Senegalese coast.

Badkhen brings a novelist's eye to her intimate chronicle as she immerses herself in community life, living and working with the fishermen and their families. Her eloquent and elegiac account offers a fascinating glimpse into a way of life that looks set to disappear along with the vanishing fish stocks. "All our hope is in the sea," says the mother of a fisherman who died at sea. But, sadly, there is little to sustain that hope.

A US journalist and author, Badkhen has spent much of her life in the global south.

Read on

At Night All Blood Is Black by David Diop (2018), translated by Anna Moschovakis; Ambiguous Adventure by Cheikh Hamidou Kane (1961), translated by Katherine Woods; The Beggars' Strike: Or, the Dregs of Society by Aminata Sow Fall (1979), translated by Dorothy S Blair; The Belly of the Atlantic by Fatou Diome (2003), translated by Lulu Norman and Ros Schwartz; The Most Secret Memory of Men: by Mohamed Mbougar Sarr (2021), translated by Lara Vergnaud.

Sierra Leone

The Memory of Love by Aminatta Forna (2010)

Forna's powerful, poignant novel of love, loss and betrayal is set either side of Sierra Leone's brutal, decade-long civil war. The tale of two love triangles, 30 years apart, unfolds against a backdrop of the country's troubled history.

In a Freetown hospital in 2001, a dying former academic, Elias Cole, is keen to reveal a past that still haunts him to a visiting

British psychologist, Adrian Lockheart. Elias's story focuses on 1969, the year of the moon landing, of his obsession with a colleague's beautiful wife, and of increasing repression in the country. In the same hospital, Adrian befriends a young, local surgeon, Kai Mansaray, who is tormented by the horrors he witnessed during the civil war in the 1990s. Adrian, who has left behind a troubled marriage and a child in England, "did not come [to Sierra Leone] expecting to find happiness". But a meeting with a young women, Mamakay, changes everything.

The plot hinges on coincidences, but these are seamlessly stitched together. The evolving tale is a slow burn that inexorably draws the reader in as its dual strands come together. Well researched, thought provoking and beautifully written, Forna's novel offers an exploration of the legacy of violence and its impact on a community.

Scottish-born Forna, a former journalist, spent part of her childhood in Sierra Leone. Her father, a dissident Sierra Leonean politician, was imprisoned and executed when she was 11.
See also: *The Devil That Danced on the Water: A Daughter's Memoir (2002); Ancestor Stones (2006); Happiness (2018)*

A Long Way Gone: The True Story of a Child Soldier by Ishmael Beah (2007)

Beah's bestselling memoir is a harrowing account of his time spent as a child soldier in Sierra Leone's civil war, one of Africa's most vicious conflicts.

When he was just 12, in 1993, Beah's village was attacked and burned by rebels from the Revolutionary United Front (RUF). Separated from his parents, he fled with a group of boys. Later, he wandered alone in the jungle for months, stalked by fear and hunger. He was finally "saved" by the army, but that safety came at a very high price. Aged 13, he was forced to join the soldiers. As a result of smoking marijuana and sniffing "brown brown" – cocaine cut with gunpowder – he became a revenge-seeking, pitiless murderer and torturer, a killing machine in a dirty war.

However, his story ends on a positive note. After three years in the army, he found rehabilitation and redemption through Unicef – and, ultimately, a new life in the US. Despite its simple, pared-down prose, Beah's story from innocent child to blood-thirsty soldier and then a return to society is eloquently told.

Both his parents and his two brothers were killed in the war. The 11-year conflict left more than 50,000 dead and permanently scarred the lives of thousands of children. Beah is now dedicated to raising awareness of the plight of child soldiers in conflicts around the world.

See also: Radiance of Tomorrow (2014)

Blood Diamonds: Tracing the Deadly Path of the World's Most Precious Stones by Greg Campbell (2002)

Sierra Leone's diamonds, first discovered in 1930, turned out to be a resource curse on steroids. The world's lust for the gems has led to deaths and displacements, and in the 1990s helped to fuel a savage, decade-long civil war. The rebel RUF, largely made up of drug-crazed teenagers, mined tens of millions of dollars' worth of gems annually to enrich warlords and buy arms and opiates as it sowed terror – looting, raping, torturing and killing. But the rebels' "signature war crime was amputation". Around 20,000 civilians had their limbs hacked off with axes and machetes.

Diamond sales funded not just the murderous RUF but also – through smugglers and shady dealers – the Lebanese group Hezbollah and the terrorist organisation al-Qaida.

Campbell's shocking, yet gripping, account of the war is based on a number of trips he made to the country in 2001, during a fragile peace. He spoke to survivors, warlords, peacekeepers and diamond miners and merchants as he bravely traversed the country. He describes Sierra Leone at that time as "a vacuum of violence, poverty, warlords and misery, a tiny corner of west Africa where the wheels have fallen completely off".

No one comes out of the tale well: neither peacekeepers from west African nations, nor the monopoly-aspiring diamond company De Beers, nor the UN, which eventually deployed its largest and most expensive peacekeeping force ever.

Campbell, an American journalist, lives in Colorado.

Read on

Beasts of No Nation by Uzodinma Iweala (2005); The Heart of the Matter by Graham Greene (1948); Moses, Citizen and Me by Delia Jarrett-Macauley (2005); The Palm Oil Stain by Nadia Maddy (2011)

Somalia

Crossbones by Nuruddin Farah (2011)

Set in Somalia around the time of the 2006 US-backed invasion by Ethiopia, the final volume in Farah's Past Imperfect trilogy can be read as a standalone novel. This absorbing story brings home the human tragedy engendered by the catastrophic fallout from a failed state.

Three members of a Somali-American family return to find their homeland imploding under an Islamist regime in control of the capital, Mogadishu, as war nears and piracy proliferates off its coast. Foreign correspondent Malik has come to write about political conflict and piracy; his father-in-law, Jeebleh, is re-establishing contact with old friends who he hopes will protect Malik and ease his path; and Malik's elder brother, Ahl, is searching for a stepson thought to have joined the Islamist militia on advice from an imam in his Minnesota hometown.

Farah skilfully evokes the paranoia and desperation that stalk the fragmented country, where trust is in short supply and good people find themselves unable to steer it away from self-destruction. This is an impassioned insider's portrayal of present-day Somalia, and of lives blighted by relentless violence and civil war.

Somalia's most famous novelist went into exile in the 1970s, during the rule of the dictator Siad Barre. He now lives in the US and South Africa, but has vowed "to keep my country alive by writing about it".

See also: Maps (1986); From a Crooked Rib (1970); North of Dawn (2018)

The Orchard of Lost Souls by Nadifa Mohamed (2013)

On the eve of the civil war in the late 1980s, two women and a girl in Hargeisa, north-western Somalia, find themselves caught up in the turbulence as their lives intersect. In this story of conflict and survival, events unfold through the eyes of Deqo, a nine-year-old orphan born and raised in a refugee camp, who ran away and is now cared for by prostitutes; Kawsar, an elderly, grieving widow bedridden after being badly beaten at a police station; and Filsan, a zealous young female soldier from Mogadishu, here to help suppress the growing rebellion against the dictatorship.

All three are wrestling with memories of lost loved ones. In a chapter on each revealing their past, Mohamed sensitively builds her cast of strong, self-empowered female characters. As the revolt grows and the army moves "not just to black out the city but to silence it", the civil war's first "orgy of violence

[is] enacted". But amid the harrowing events taking place, the author inserts a ray of hope.

Mohamed's novel certainly succeeds in achieving her stated goal of "[elucidating] Somali history for a wider audience". Born in Hargeisa (now in Somaliland), she came to Britain as a five-year-old with her family – a temporary move that became permanent as a result of the civil war.

See also: Black Mamba Boy (2010); The Fortune Men (2021)

The World's Most Dangerous Place: Inside the Outlaw State of Somalia by James Fergusson (2013)

Beyond the attention-seeking title is a perceptive and engaging account of Somalia's descent into violence and lawlessness. The country has not had a properly functioning central government since the overthrow of the dictator Siad Barre in 1991. Meanwhile, it has seen seemingly endless clan warfare, an Islamist insurgency, foreign military interventions, famine, pervasive corruption, piracy and – unsurprisingly – the flight of some 2 million people abroad.

The civil war is known locally as "the destruction", and one source tells the author that wherever the four horsemen of the apocalypse ride out to in the world, they return nightly to stable in Somalia. Fergusson bravely travels within Somalia and elsewhere, also visiting the peaceful but unrecognised Republic of Somaliland; the breakaway region of Puntland, home to a lucrative piracy industry; and the Somali diaspora in the US and UK.

Alongside his reportage he explores the backstory essential to understanding how the country gained its unenviable reputation as "the world's most failed state", and why peace and security in Somalia matter far beyond its borders.

Fergusson detects reasons for optimism, with the al-Qaida-affiliated al-Shabaab Islamists in retreat, piracy reduced, bustling markets, Somalis returning from abroad, and politics and law and order slowly re-emerging. The author is a British journalist and foreign correspondent.

See also: In Search of the River Jordan: A Story of Palestine, Israel and the Struggle for Water (2023)

Read on

Born in the Big Rains: A Memoir of Somalia and Survival by Fadumo Korn with Sabine Eichhorst (2006), translated by Tobe Levin; Tale of Boon's Wife by Fartumo Kusow (2017); Getting Somalia Wrong? Faith, War and Hope in a Shattered State by Mary Harper (2012)

South Africa

Disgrace by JM Coetzee (1999)

A twice-divorced, fiftysomething Capetown University professor has an affair with one of his female students. A complaint is made about his transgression – and he is sacked. Thus disgraced, David

Lurie retreats to his daughter Lucy's remote farm in Eastern Cape for reflection and redemption.

At first, it seems rural life may offer some form of solace, and he busies himself with writing an opera about Lord Byron. But an attack on the farm by three black men brings into sharp relief the changing balance of power between the races in post-apartheid South Africa and further complicates the strained relationship between father and daughter. Is this the price whites have to pay for staying on? Must they "humble [themselves] before history" to atone for past misdeeds under apartheid?

Freighted with his literary hallmarks of ambiguity and bleakness, Coetzee offers a deeply pessimistic view of the "rainbow nation". Disgrace doesn't merely attach to David. There's the disgrace of what happens to Lucy during the attack, the disgrace of violence and crime in the new South Africa, and the disgrace of apartheid. Although this Booker prize-winning novel is both controversial and disturbing, its taut, sparse narrative – in David's voice – is quietly propulsive.

Coetzee, who also won the Booker for Life & Times of Michael K, was awarded the Nobel prize for literature in 2003. The South African author emigrated to Australia in 2002.

See also: Life & Times of Michael K (1983); Waiting for the Barbarians (1980); Age of Iron (1990)

Bitter Fruit by Achmat Dangor (2001)

Silas Ali, a former African National Congress activist working as a lawyer with the Truth and Reconciliation Commission in the post-apartheid 1990s, runs into the white policeman who raped his wife 20 years ago while Silas was handcuffed in the back of the police van. It sets off a train of events that causes Silas's family to slowly fall apart.

Set at the tail end of Nelson Mandela's presidency, the novel follows a trajectory of memory, confession and retribution, exploring how South Africa struggles to transcend the damaging legacy of its contorted past. "There are certain things people do not forget or forgive," a character in the story says. "Rape is one of them."

The fragile relations between Silas, his wife Lydia and their 19-year-old son Mikey, a "coloured", middle-class family living in Johannesburg, unravel under the strain of confronting the rape. Lydia's two-decades-long repressed grief and anger surfaces; and when Mikey, on secretly reading his mother's diary, learns of her violation, the already conflicted young man also discovers he is its "bitter fruit".

Dangor's intimate and intelligently crafted story draws the reader into the family's – and the country's – angst. It's a sad, lingering tale that portrays a world unfamiliar to many western readers.

Johannesburg-born Dangor, who died in 2020, was politically active both under apartheid and after it ended.

See also: The Z Town Trilogy (1990)

Winnie & Nelson: Portrait of a Marriage by Jonny Steinberg (2023)

Steinberg's richly rendered interwoven biography offers a fascinating insight not only into the turbulent marriage of South Africa's most iconic couple, but also into the country's tortured path to freedom. The union of Nelson Mandela and Winnie Madikizela-Mandela became a "national institution", and it symbolised both the aspirations and the deep fissures within the anti-apartheid struggle. The book chronicles the couple's early lives, their relationship, their long, enforced separation with Nelson's incarceration, and their divorce.

Winnie & Nelson is a page turner as the author's diligent research, including access to previously unreleased material, brings new and compelling revelations. Though Steinberg lauds the couple's heroism in the face of tyranny, he doesn't hide their flaws. The intimate portraits lift the veil on both the saintly Nelson and the forceful Winnie and, although the author is empathetic, he doesn't shy away from some of the pair's more unsavoury behaviour, especially the latter's descent into violence, intemperance and corruption.

The fairytale marriage cracked under the strain of the apartheid regime's horrific repression, with Nelson spending 27 years in jail and Winnie subjected to relentless surveillance, torture, exile and ostracism. For the Mandelas, political triumph was embraced by personal tragedy. "The myth of their tale is necessary," Steinberg concludes. "So, too, is the illumination of their human frailty." The South African author is a writer and academic who has lectured at Oxford and Yale universities.

See also: Three Letter Plague: A Young Man's Journey Through a Great Epidemic (2008)

Read on

The Conservationist by Nadine Gordimer (1974); The Promise by Damian Galgut (2021); In Corner B by Es'kia Mphahlele (1967); You Will Be Safe Here by Damian Barr (2019); Innards by Magogodi oaMphela Makhene (2023); These Are Not Gentle People by Andrew Harding (2020); After Mandela: The Struggle for Freedom in Post-Apartheid South Africa by Douglas Foster (2012); Dry White Season by André Brink (1979); Red Dust by Gillian Slovo (2000); Ways of Dying by Zakes Mda (1995); Long Walk to Freedom by Nelson Mandela (1994)

Sudan

Season of Migration to the North by Tayeb Salih (1966), translated by Denys Johnson-Davies

After several years studying in Europe, the young, unnamed narrator returns to his "small village at the bend of the Nile", eager to play his part in the new, post-colonial Sudan. At home he meets a mysterious stranger, Mustafa Sa'eed, who had also lived abroad many years earlier.

The two men are drawn together, and the story of Sa'eed's life in London is revealed in fragments of reminiscences and writings. Though feted for his intellect and pursued by European women, Sa'eed is ultimately overpowered by events that lead to his undoing – and his return to Sudan.

One day Sa'eed suddenly disappears, presumed drowned in the Nile, leaving his new friend to look after his wife and children. The young man, faced with making difficult decisions, finds himself caught between Africa and Europe, tradition and modernity. At the same time, he grows increasingly disillusioned with the changes in his own country and with "the new rulers of Africa".

Salih's lyrical, bleak and idiosyncratic novel of social and cultural conflict between coloniser and colonised is regarded as one of the finest in Arab literature. However, its sexually explicit passages and political content have seen it banned on and off in various Arab countries, including his native Sudan. Salih himself spent many years abroad, working for the BBC in London and Unesco in Paris. He died in 2009.

See also: The Wedding of Zein and Other Stories (1962), translated by Denys Johnson-Davies

Lyrics Alley by Leila Aboulela (2010)

Set in 1950s Khartoum, Aboulela's novel follows the fortunes of the rich and powerful Abouzeid family. As Sudan slips from the grasp of both Britain and Egypt and heads for independence, the family – together with the country – faces the challenges of a changing world.

The family patriarch, Mahmoud, a successful businessman, lives in two worlds, symbolised by his wives: one Sudanese, traditional and uneducated, the other Egyptian, much younger and progressive. Mahmoud's younger son Nur – the deft and dashing heir to the family business – and his niece Soraya are very much in love, and a glittering future awaits them. But their plans are destroyed and Mahmoud is left devastated "in a twist which Fate had hidden", after Nur is paralysed in a swimming accident.

As Nur struggles to rebuild his life, growing tensions lead to war breaking out between Mahmoud's wives – a collision between the past and the future – and family members are caught in the crossfire. Aboulela's elegant and assured storytelling, and her complex, well-crafted characters make this an absorbing family saga. She was born in Cairo and grew up in Khartoum. Lyrics Alley was inspired by the life of her uncle Hassan Awad Aboulela, a Sudanese poet and lyricist, who was paralysed after a freak accident.

See also: Minaret (2005); River Spirit (2023)

Sudan: Darfur and the Failure of an African State by Richard Cockett (2010/2015)

At independence from Britain in 1956, Sudan stood on the brink of a promising future. Instead, Africa's largest country descended into civil war – between the Arab-Muslim north and the black-Christian south – and catastrophically imploded. Khartoum's indifference to the remote regions, and the centralising of power and economic benefits, sparked rebellions in the south and east, and in Darfur in the west.

Over the years the government became more Islamic and increasingly repressive – exacerbating religious and ethnic divides. A nadir was reached following atrocities in Darfur, where government-backed Arab militias were accused of ethnic cleansing. The on-off 50-year civil war claimed more than 2 million lives before a peace agreement was signed in 2005, leading to the south's secession. In 2009, President Omar al-Bashir was indicted for war crimes by the international criminal court. Bashir was ousted in 2019.

In this informative, eminently readable history and analysis of Sudan's failure as a state, Cockett draws on interviews with many of the main players. He liberally apportions blame for Sudan's anarchy and impoverishment, citing "meddling western politicians … spineless African leaders, shamelessly silent Muslim countries … and myopic Sudanese politicians". Sadly, optimism for the future is in short supply: "Sudan was born in blood and has yet to learn another way to live."

Cockett is a senior editor at the Economist and a member of the Institute for Advanced Study at Princeton University.
See also: Blood, Dreams and Gold: The Changing Face of Burma by Richard Cockett (2015)

Read on

What Is the What by Dave Eggers (2006); A Line in the River: Khartoum, City of Memory by Jamal Mahjoub (2018); They Poured Fire on Us From the Sky: The True Story of Three Lost Boys from Sudan by Benson Deng, Alephonsion Deng, Benjamin Ajak with Judy A Bernstein (2005); A Mouth Full of Salt by Reem Gaafar (2024); Something is Going to Fall Like Rain by Ros Wynne-Jones (2009); Cities without Palms by Tarek Eltayeb (2009), translated by Kareem James Abu-Zeid

Tanzania

Afterlives by Abdulrazak Gurnah (2020)

In his ninth novel Gurnah weaves together historical facts and fiction to paint a vivid picture of German rule in east Africa at the beginning of the 20th century. The Germans are brutal masters, employing their colonial army of native mercenaries to sow terror among the population. As Gurnah writes: "This was a time when [the] land was soaked in blood and littered with corpses."

He masterfully chronicles the lives of four main characters: Khalifa, an Indian-African bookkeeper who works for a local businessman; Ilyas, who is kidnapped as a child by the Germans, then educated by them and later volunteers to join the colonial troops; his sister Afiya, who, after her parents disappear, is taken in by a couple who treat her appallingly; and Hamza, who is sold into bondage by his parents but flees to join the colonial *schutz-truppe*, a decision he quickly regrets. Their lives are interwoven as they strive to find their place in a region (today's Tanzania) shackled by colonialism and torn apart by the first world war

In this quietly compelling novel, Gurnah, a superb storyteller, delivers a powerful indictment of colonialism, shining a light on a forgotten slice of history. The Zanzibar-born author fled the island for the UK in 1968, aged 17, four years after an armed revolt followed independence from Britain. He was awarded the Nobel prize for literature in 2021.

See also: By the Sea (2001); Theft (2025); Paradise (1994); Gravel Heart (2017)

The Book of Secrets by MG Vassanji (1994)

The eponymous book is the diary of a British colonial officer, Alfred Corbin, whose first posting was in the fictional town of Kikono, near German East Africa on the Kenya-Tanganyika border, in 1913. In 1980s Dar es Salaam, Pius Fernandes, a retired schoolteacher, is given the diary by one of his former students. With his interest piqued by its contents – "It is a magic bottle, this book, full of captured spirits" – Fernandes is driven to investigate and "breathe life" into the characters contained in it.

With a focus on the immigrant Indian community in east Africa, what follows is a sweeping saga across seven decades, spanning colonial rule, two world wars, independence in the 1960s, and political and racial tensions. Vassanji meshes the past and the present as he chronicles history and social mores, linked in with an abiding mystery. The seductive tale flits across generations through three main characters: Miriam, a beautiful and mysterious Indian woman who works as Corbin's maid for a time; her shopkeeper husband Pipa, who is unsure whether he is the father of their son Ali; and Ali himself, who is unusually fair with grey eyes.

Towards the end of the novel, Fernandes contemplates the reducing circumstances of his fellow expatriates: "We were immensely aware of our essential homelessness. Our world was diminishing with the empire."

Vassanji grew up in Kenya and Tanzania, and now lives in Canada.

See also: The Magic of Saida (2012); And Home Was Kariakoo: A Memoir of East Africa (2014); The Gunny Sack (1989)

Revolution in Zanzibar: An American's Cold War Tale by Don Petterson (2002)

Barely a month after independence from Britain in 1964, Zanzibar erupted in Marxist-inspired bloody revolution and found itself in the eye of a cold-war storm. Smouldering ethnic hatreds surfaced as rebels from the disgruntled African majority rose up against their Omani Arab rulers. The ensuing killing spree left 5,000 people – mostly Arabs – dead. For a brief time the turbulent events preoccupied both the British prime minister and the US president, who feared the "cancer of communism" could spread from the spice island to mainland Africa.

Pettersen, who was working at the US mission in Zanzibar, was the only American to remain on the island throughout the conflict. Although seen through a pro-US prism, his engrossing eyewitness account provides a fascinating insight into the political climate and social upheaval. He tells of the political machinations – both foreign and local – the intricacies of US foreign policy and the everyday life of a diplomat during a tumultuous period in the east African island's history.

He also sheds light on the to-ing and fro-ing with neighbouring Tanganyika and the dilemmas, decisions and doings of its president, Julius Nyerere. Within months of the revolution the Zanzibari leadership signed up to a union with Tanganiyka to form what became Tanzania.

A career diplomat, Pettersen served as US ambassador to a number of African countries during his near four decades with the Foreign Service.

Read on

Julius Nyerere by Paul Bjerk (2017); Zanzibar Uhuru: Revolution, Two Women and the Challenge of Survival by Anne M Chappel (2015); Zanzibar by Giles Foden (2002); A Modern History of Tanganyika by John Ilife (1979)

Uganda

Kintu by Jennifer Nansubuga Makumbi (2014)

Makumbi's magisterial family saga comes trailing accolades – and deservedly so. The story, which arcs across generations, begins in 2004 as a mob beats Kamu Kintu to death in a Kampala slum. It then jumps back to 1750 as an ancestor, regional governor Kintu Kidda, leads a delegation on an arduous journey to pledge loyalty to the new Buganda king. On the way, he accidentally kills his adopted son, which leads to a curse being unleashed on the Kintu clan by the boy's biological father.

A vast, deftly drawn cast of characters is presented, many dogged by the curse that plagues the clan down the generations. The novel focuses on four descendants and their family branches, through to modern-day Uganda, as they struggle with poverty, violence, HIV/Aids, social mores and relationships. The story's various strands are satisfyingly drawn together in the final chapter as clan members gather on their ancestral land in 2004 to try to break the curse.

Both clan and country are vividly chronicled in this inventive novel which, despite its epic scale, achieves intimacy. Mukumbi mined her native Uganda's rich history and culture for this bold, ambitious debut – hailed as the great Ugandan novel – and it marks the arrival of an immensely gifted author. Mukumbi, who grew up in Uganda, now lives in the UK.

See also: The First Woman (2020); Manchester Happened (2019);
A Girl Is a Body of Water (2020)

Abyssinian Chronicles by Moses Isegawa (1998)

The Marquezian opening sentence reels the reader right into Isegawa's exuberant debut novel: "Three final images flashed across Serenity's mind as he disappeared into the jaws of the colossal crocodile …" The narrator, Mugezi, comes of age alongside his country in a story set against the bloody political turmoil of post-colonial Uganda in the 1970s and 1980s, after the British had "[escaped] the flames of the house they had set on fire".

Through the fortunes of three generations of his extended family, Mugezi weaves together the personal and political to also tell the story of Uganda, punctuated by religious and tribal divisions, dictatorship, the expulsion of Indians, guerrilla wars and the scourge of HIV/Aids. The main setting is during the regime of Idi Amin, who terrorised Ugandans between 1971 and 1979. While his country struggles to shake itself free from despotism, the young narrator strives to be free of his tyrannical parents – an oppressive father and fanatically Roman Catholic mother. Mugezi is a survivor – and a wise, witty and acerbic storyteller – who is prepared to do what it takes to come safely through the turbulent times.

Isegawa's vibrant, elegant prose makes this a novel to savour. Moses Isegawa is the nom de plume of Kampala-born Sey Wava, who worked as a teacher before emigrating to the Netherlands in 1990, aged 27. He returned to his native Uganda in 2006.

See also: Snakepit (2004)

The Teeth May Smile But the Heart Does Not Forget: Memory and Murder in Uganda by Andrew Rice (2009)

In 1972, during Idi Amin's bloody eight-year reign, a local leader with ties to the opposition disappeared. Thirty years later, Eliphaz Laki's son Duncan finds a clue that leads to three former soldiers – including Amin's top army general – being indicted for his father's murder.

Rice uses Duncan's pursuit of justice for his father, one of thousands killed under Amin's dictatorship, to tell the larger story of Uganda's recent tortuous past. Deftly meshing reportage with history, The Teeth May Smile reads like a riveting murder mystery.

The country's "deforming" colonial period, marked by British divide and rule, left Uganda at independence in 1962 riven by political, religious and ethnic differences. During the post-colonial years disagreement and discord metastasise into violence and repression, leading to a "looping litany of vengeance" that casts a long shadow to this day.

Beyond the unfolding murder trial, the book also explores the wider issue of forgiving and forgetting in a country haunted by its history. This well-researched and sharply observed account paints a flesh-and-blood portrait of Uganda, and serves as an excellent primer on the nation. The title comes from a proverb of Laki's Banyankole tribe.

US journalist Rice spent four years following the trial and traversing the country doing research for his book.

Read on

We Are All Birds of Uganda by Hafsa Zayyan (2021); The Last King of Scotland by Giles Foden (1998); Tropical Fish: Tales from Entebbe by Doreen Baingana (2005); The Night Wanderers: Uganda's Children and the Lord's Resistance Army by Wojciech Jagielski (2012), translated by Antonia Lloyd-Jones; Kololo Hill by Neema Shah (2021)

Zimbabwe

Nervous Conditions by Tsitsi Dangarembga (1988)

Dangarembga's beautifully crafted bildungsroman, set in late-1960s, white-ruled Rhodesia, explores colonialism, racism and sexism, offering a captivating insight into the lives of those "with the poverty of blackness on one side and the weight of woman-hood on the other".

From the memorable opening line – "I was not sorry when my brother died" – the story never lets up. It turns out that Tambu, the novel's 14-year-old narrator from a dirt-poor Shona family, has good reasons for the insouciance to her brother's demise.

His death also enables her to receive an education – initially denied in favour of her male sibling – and embark on a path to emancipation from poverty and patriarchy.

The teenager's family relies on the generosity of her uncle Babamakuru, who is the headmaster of a black mission school. Tambu goes to live with him and attend his school. There she grows close to her cousin Nyasha, Babamakuru's daughter, who is struggling to fit back into traditional Shona culture after living with her parents in England. Both teenagers are trying to find their way in the world – a journey fraught with conflicts and unforeseen consequences.

This superb debut novel is widely regarded as a classic of African literature. Dangarembga, a Zimbabwean writer, film-maker and playwright, portrayed Tambu's later life in two sequels. *See also: The Book of Not (2006); This Mournable Body (2018)*

Elegy for Easterly by Petina Gappah (2009)

Gappah's lauded short story collection offers 13 incisive snapshots of contemporary Zimbabwe. A widow watches, alongside the president, as her husband is buried with full military honours – but the coffin contains stones rather than his body; Easterly, a shanty town in which houses "erupted without City permission" is razed to the ground by government bulldozers; a young bride doesn't know her husband has HIV/Aids, though the wedding guests do; a family waits at the airport for a relative's body to arrive from the UK; a furniture factory worker, "retired" without a pension, literally dances his life away.

Mugabe's shadow looms over these stories of ordinary people struggling to get on with their lives as they are buffeted by hyperinflation, hypocrisy, corruption and HIV/Aids. As one protagonist says: "Before the president [Mugabe] was elected, the Zimbabwe ruins were a prehistoric monument in Masvingo province. Now, the Zimbabwe ruins extend to the whole country."

Told with vim and vigour, the tales – though mostly tragic – are suffused with sparkling humour and peppered with the Shona language. The elegy is not just for Easterly, but for a Zimbabwe the author once knew. She says she wrote the stories "out of rage and hopelessness" as her country went into meltdown under Mugabe. Gappah worked for more than a decade as an international trade lawyer in Geneva.

See also: The Book of Memory (2015); Rotten Row (2016)

The Fear: The Last Days of Mugabe by Peter Godwin (2010)

In 2008, the president lost an election and Godwin flew back to his native Zimbabwe planning to "dance on Robert Mugabe's political grave". But instead of relinquishing control after almost three decades in power, the 84-year-old dictator and his henchmen unleashed a wave of vicious beatings, rape, torture and killings against supporters of the opposition Movement for Democratic Change.

The "abuse on an industrial scale" left shattered limbs and broken lives. Zimbabweans called the period "The Fear", and it brought to mind the 1981 massacre in Matabeleland when Mugabe's forces attacked his former allies, leaving more than 20,000 civilians dead. Meanwhile, seizures of farmland by black, self-proclaimed "war veterans" disrupted food production and plunged the country – already facing economic devastation – deeper into misery. On Mugabe's watch what was once the bread basket of Africa had become an economic basket case.

As "stenographer to [the] suffering", Godwin bears witness to the horrific violence, and marvels at the incredible courage and resilience of those who continued to resist Mugabe. His unflinching account of the violence is a demanding read. But also compelling, as he delivers a searing indictment of the regime and tries to understand what happened to the country he was born and grew up in. Godwin, a journalist and memoirist, lives in New York.

See also: When a Crocodile Eats the Sun (2006); Mukiwa: A White Boy in Africa (1996)

Read on

We Need New Names by NoViolet Bulawayo (2013); Two Weeks in November: The Astonishing Untold Story of the Operation That Toppled Mugabe by Douglas Rogers (2013); The Hairdresser of Harare by Tendai Huchu (2010); Don't Let's Go to the Dogs Tonight by Alexandra Fuller (2001); The Uncertainty of Hope by Valerie

Tagwira (2006); House of Stone by Novuyo Rosa Tshuma (2018); The Stone Virgins by Yvonne Vera (2002); Harvest of Thorns by Shimmer Chinodya (1989)

Africa general

The Looting Machine: Warlords, Tycoons, Smugglers and the Systematic Theft of Africa's Wealth by Tom Burgis (2015)

A powerful exposé of dirty business in Africa – the pillage of the continent's resources by corrupt officials, businesspeople, kleptocratic leaders and multinationals that leaves poverty, violence and repression in its wake.

Born in Blackness: Africa, Africans, and the Making of the Modern World, 1471 to the Second World War by Howard W French (2021)

French, a journalist and academic, sweeps across six centuries, putting Africa's story – often relegated to the margins of history – at the heart of shaping the world that we live in.

See also: China's Second Continent: How a Million Migrants Are Building a New Empire in Africa (2014)

Africa: Altered States, Ordinary Miracles by Richard Dowden (2008/2019)

Dowden, a journalist and former executive director of the Royal African Society who has travelled widely and reported extensively on Africa, offers an insightful, empathetic and very readable overview of the changing continent.

Read on

The Scramble for Africa by Thomas Pakenham (1990); The Shadow of the Sun: My African Life by Ryszard Kapuscinski (1998), translated by Klara Glowczewska; A Fistful of Shells: West Africa from the Rise of the Slave Trade to the Age of Revolution by Toby Green (2019); How to Write About Africa by Binyavanga Wainaina (2006); An African History of Africa: From the Dawn of Humanity to Independence by Zeinab Badawi (2024)

Middle East and North Africa

Algeria

What the Day Owes the Night by Yasmina Khadra (2008), translated by Frank Wynne

Khadra's novel of an Arab boy growing up in 20th-century French Algeria is an epic tale of family, love and war. The narrator, Younes, is the son of a poor Arab farmer who loses his land and, in search of work, drags the family to a slum in the city of Oran. The father, ground down by poverty, eventually agrees for Younes to be brought up by his uncle, an educated and affluent pharmacist.

It's a life-changing experience for the young boy who, renamed Jonas, moves with his new family to the town of Rio Salado, where he goes to school among Europeans. Jonas acquires a tight coterie of friends, but anti-Arab racism, both subtle and overt, is never far away. The group's friendship is sorely tested by the arrival of a beautiful young woman, Emilie, from whom they learn how much love can hurt. But their camaraderie faces a much greater challenge as Algeria's grisly war of independence reaches Rio Salado and racial tensions erupt.

Jonas's idyllic life is shattered by the bitter conflict, and he finds himself forced to take sides – to choose between an Algerian or European identity. This rich, captivating novel offers Younes/Jonas as an acute observer of both colonial and colonised Algeria.

Yasmina Khadra is the pen name of Mohammed Moulesse-houl, a former Algerian army officer who adopted his wife's name to evade military censors. He lives in France.

See also: *Wolf Dreams* (1999), translated by Linda Black; *The Angels Die* (2016), translated by Howard Curtis; *The Swallows Of Kabul* (2002), translated by John Cullen

Fantasia by Assia Djebar (1985), translated by Dorothy S Blair

In the first novel of her Algerian quartet, Djebar weaves together the autobiographical story of a young girl's coming of age with the history of her country's colonisation by France in 1830 and the war of independence in the 1950s. She uses a colourful mix of fictional and factual history to counter colonial as well as patriarchal attitudes – at times reflecting how much the two have in common.

The novel emphasises the role played by Algerian women in society and in the country's history, not only through their suffering but also through their tenacity and resilience. In the latter part of the book a chorus of female voices tells of women's experiences – as rebel fighters, victims of torture, exiles – in the vicious liberation struggle against France.

In raw, emotional prose the narrator recounts the stories of women struggling to gain both Algeria's independence and their own. She says she is "writing ... above all, to resurrect so many vanished sisters". This unconventional novel's elaborate construction can be frustrating at times, but it presents a memorable account of lives lived under French repression.

Assia Djebar was the pen name of the Algerian novelist, academic and film-maker Fatima-Zohra Imalayen, who lived in

France and was elected to the prestigious Académie Française in 2005. She died in 2015.

See also: The Tongue's Blood Does Not Run Dry: Algerian Stories (1997), translated by Tegan Raleigh

Algeria: Anger of the Dispossessed by Martin Evans and John Phillips (2007)

After a long and bloody war to end French colonial rule, independent Algeria emerged in 1962 to become a darling of the non-aligned movement. But, as Evans and Phillips reveal, beneath the veneer of a revolutionary, progressive state lurked a repressive and increasingly corrupt military dictatorship.

The unemployed, disenfranchised and alienated post-independence generation, meanwhile, found itself at odds with the official myths of Algeria's glorious liberation struggle. Pent-up anger exploded on to the streets in 1988's Black October, and the protests were harshly suppressed. As many young Algerians turned to political Islam in their search for solutions, the government tried, and failed, to contain the movement. Violence escalated, and the regime in desperation called elections in 1991. But when the Islamists looked like winning, the military promptly cancelled the vote.

The ugly civil war that ensued – in which unspeakable atrocities were committed by both sides – lasted more than a decade, claiming around 200,000 lives. The violence has subsided but, say the authors, Algeria's agony is not yet over. The "anger of the dispossessed" remains, and it is "a fury that has the potential to endure for decades to come". There's much to be praised in this cogent and clear-eyed political history, which offers a fascinating insight into Algeria's opaque politics.

Evans is a historian at Sussex University, and Phillips is a journalist who reported on Algeria for the Times newspaper.

Read on

The Star of Algiers by Aziz Chouaki (2005), translated by Ros Schwartz and Lulu Norman; The Lovers of Algeria by Anouar Benmalek (2001), translated by Joanna Kilmartin; Harraga by Boualem Sansal (2015), translated by Frank Wynne; The Meursault Investigation by Kamel Daoud (2013), translated by John Cullen

Egypt

Palace Walk by Naguib Mahfouz (1956), translated by William Maynard Hutchins and Olive E Kenny

Palace Walk is the first novel in Mahfouz's sumptuous Cairo trilogy, a three-generation family saga set in the early 20th century. The trilogy, regarded as his magnum opus, runs from after the first world war to Gamal Abdel Nasser's overthrow of the ancien regime in 1952. The rich, intense story offers an inside view of modern Egypt as the country attempts to emerge from British occupation and forge its own identity. Palace Walk tells the story up to the 1919 revolution against the British.

Al-Sayyid Ahmad Abd al-Jawad, a prosperous merchant, rules over his wife, three sons and two daughters with an iron hand. He runs his family strictly according to Qur'anic principles and demands unquestioning obedience. But his own behaviour is far from irreproachable as he indulges his desires for fine wine and full-figured women. Mahfouz paints an intimate portrait of the Jawads with humour and close attention to detail. Their trials and tribulations reflect the strife in a changing Egypt. As the country struggles to end colonial rule, the Jawad children battle to break free from their father's tyrannical control.

Mahfouz, the Arab world's most celebrated novelist, won the Nobel prize for literature in 1988. He survived an assassination attempt by Islamists in 1994, which caused permanent injury and forced him to live with bodyguards. He died in 2006.
See also: Palace of Desire (1957); Sugar Street (1957), both translated by William Maynard Hutchins and Angele Botros Samaan; Midaq Alley (1947), translated by Trevor LeGassick

The Yacoubian Building by Alaa Al Aswany (2002), translated by Humphrey Davies

Sex and the city loom large in the lives of the Yacoubian building's inhabitants. The once grand, now decaying apartment block in central Cairo houses a rich cast of characters, whose stories Aswany weaves together to portray contemporary Egyptian life.

The taboo-busting novel tells of Cairo's residents going about their lives and coming up against corruption, police brutality, sexism, homophobia and religious extremism – all seething under the surface of President Hosni Mubarak's sclerotic regime. Among the bustling building's residents are poor squatters living on the roof, an ageing playboy nostalgic for a bygone era, a gay newspaper editor in love with a policeman, a bitter doorkeeper's son who turns to militant Islam, and a woman who puts up with sexual harassment at work so that she can keep her job and support her family. The novel, reflecting people's daily frustrations in a society where money and influence are prized above all else, offers a damning indictment of the powers that be.

A dentist by profession, Aswany opened his first clinic in Cairo's real-life Yacoubian building. He says dentistry is his "window on Egyptian society" – a window that spurred him to write one of the best-selling novels in the Arab world. He took part in the 2011 Arab spring protests and since 2019 has been living in self-imposed exile abroad.

See also: The Republic of False Truths (2018), translated by SR Fellowes; The Automobile Club of Egypt (2015), translated by Russell Harris; Friendly Fire (2009), translated by Humphrey Davies

Egypt on the Brink: From Nasser to the Muslim Brotherhood by Tarek Osman (2010/2013)

Egyptian writer and commentator Osman provides the backstory on why people took to the streets to oust Mubarak in 2011. He casts a shrewd eye over the six decades since Nasser's 1952 revolution, sizing up all the main players – Islamists, liberal capitalists, Coptic Christians, the army and young Egyptians. The last are a force to be reckoned with: the almost three-quarters of the population aged under 35 provided the "fuel for the revolt" that toppled Mubarak.

Nasser galvanised national – and Arab – pride, but ultimately failed to deliver on what was promised. Instead, he created "a suffocating military bureaucratic system ... [and] Egypt remained throughout [Anwar] Sadat's and Mubarak's administrations at heart a police state with a sad human rights record". Egypt's patrons in Washington – the country is the biggest recipient of US aid in the Middle East after Israel – chose to turn a blind eye to the sham democracy because of the oft-raised spectre of the Muslim Brotherhood seizing power and forming a hostile Islamist regime.

So, has Egypt seen off its last strongman? Disturbingly – and presciently – Osman says: "There is much in Egyptian history and traditions that predisposes Egyptians to expect and accept authoritarian rule." Osman is an Egyptian author, political economist, columnist and broadcaster.

Read on

Woman at Point Zero by Nawal El Saadawi (1973), translated by Sherif Hetata; The Open Door by Latifa Al-Zayyat (1960), translated by Marilyn Booth; The City Always Wins by Omar Robert Hamilton (2017); The Egyptians: A Radical Story by Jack Shenker (2016); The Nile: Downriver Through Egypt's Past and Present by Toby Wilkinson (2014); Beer in the Snooker Club by Waguih Ghali (1964); The Map of Love by Ahdaf Soueif (1999); Sunset Oasis by Bahaa Taher (2006), translated by Humphrey Davies

Iran

My Father's Notebook by Kader Abdolah (2006), translated by Susan Massotty

Abdolah's autobiographical novel sees Iran's recent history through the eyes of a father and son. Aga Akbar, who is deaf and mute, becomes a master carpet repairer. In a cave in Saffron Mountain, near where he lives, he is shown a 3,000-year-old script, which he decides to use to express himself in a notebook.

As Akbar's son Ishmael grows up, he comes to serve as his father's ears, mouth and principal link with the world. While the father is a silent witness to events taking place in the country, the son becomes a protagonist.

After the shah is overthrown in 1979, and hopes of freedom are dashed under Ayatollah Khomeini's Islamic regime, Ishmael is increasingly involved in the underground opposition. As repression intensifies, his clandestine party is "shattered like an earthenware pot that falls to the ground" and he is forced to flee the country. Years later, during his exile in Europe, Ishmael recovers his father's notebook. The story of both characters and their beloved Iran unfolds as the son gradually deciphers his father's writings from the ancient script. This poignant, affectionate and beautifully told tale reflects a longing for a lost homeland.

Hossein Sadjadi Ghaemmaghami Farahani writes under the pen name Kader Abdolah to honour two friends killed under the Islamic regime. The author, a political exile, lives in the Netherlands and writes in Dutch.

See also: The House of the Mosque (2005), translated by Susan Massotty; The King (2014), translated by Nancy Forest-Flier

My Uncle Napoleon by Iraj Pezeshkzad (1973), translated by Dick Davis

This riotous tale, set in Tehran in the early 1940s, depicts the lives of a large extended family ruled over by a despotic, deluded and paranoid patriarch, Dear Uncle Napoleon. The novel's unnamed 13-year-old narrator has a crush on his cousin, Dear Uncle's daughter, but the dysfunctional family's personalities, politics and feuds frustrate young love at every turn.

Dear Uncle hero-worships Napoleon Bonaparte, and is prone to telling extremely tall tales – which are backed up by his loyal manservant – of his own valour in battles against Britain and its allies. When British troops land in Iran at the start of the second world war, Dear Uncle is certain that perfidious Albion, whose hidden hand he sees behind almost every event, is bent on revenge against him.

This sharp and endearing satire is highly critical of the society it portrays, sending up class snobbery, family honour, personal pride and sexual shenanigans ("going to San Francisco", as a womanising uncle calls the latter). The novel is one of the most popular books in Iran and is regarded as a national treasure. Despite that, the mullahs banned it after the 1979 revolution, along with the immensely popular TV series it spawned.

Pezeshkzad, a former Iranian judge and diplomat, now lives in France.

Revolutionary Iran by Michael Axworthy (2013)

"Iran is less a country than a continent, more a civilisation than a nation," says Axworthy at the beginning of this masterful history of the Islamic Republic. His lucid and literate account takes us from the origins of the 1979 revolution that toppled the shah and installed Khomeini to President Mahmoud Ahmadinejad's hotly disputed re-election in 2009, which brought protesters on to the streets.

Iran is a big player in the Middle East and beyond, but relations between Tehran and the west are dogged by myths, misunderstandings and mistrust. The 1979 crisis, when students took US embassy staff hostage after the shah's overthrow, led "Iran into a twilight zone of diplomatic breakdown and international isolation". The country's nuclear ambitions and ongoing western sanctions have done little to change that. But, as Axworthy explains, Iran has good reasons not to trust the west: among them a US- and British-engineered coup that ousted an elected prime minister in 1953, support for the shah's repressive rule, and backing for Saddam Hussein in the eight-year Iran-Iraq war.

Although no apologist for the regime – which, as he points out, imprisons, tortures and kills political opponents – the author's reasoned and knowledgeable narrative appeals for diplomacy and understanding. Axworthy, an academic and a former head of the British Foreign Office's Iran section, died in 2019.

See also:*Iran: Empire of the Mind: A History from Zoroaster to the Present Day (2007)*

Read on

Aria by Nazanine Hozar (2019); What Iranians Want: Women, Life, Freedom by Arash Azizi (2024); Reading Lolita in Tehran: A Memoir in Books by Azar Nafisi (2003); The Cypress Tree by Kamin Mohammadi (2011); The Septembers of Shiraz by Dalia Sofer (2007); Iran's Rise and Rivalry with the US in the Middle East by Mohsen M Milani (2025); City of Lies: Love, Sex, Death and the Search for Truth in Tehran by Ramita Navai (2014); Iran Awakening: A Memoir of Revolution and Hope by Shirin Ebadi (2006), with Azadeh Moaveni; Children of the Jacaranda Tree by Sahar Delijani (2013); All the Shah's Men: An American Coup and of Middle East Terror by Stephen Kinzer (2003); The Book of Fate by Parinoush Saniee (2003), translated by Sara Khalili

Iraq

The President's Gardens by Muhsin al-Ramli (2012), translated by Luke Leafgren

From its attention-grabbing opening sentence – "In a land without bananas, the village awoke to nine banana crates, each containing the severed head of one of its sons" – Ramli's novel takes the reader on a gripping journey through Saddam Hussein's Iraq.

Fact meets fiction in this story of three friends from the same village whose lives are blighted by Iraq's turbulent history from the 1980s Iran-Iraq war to the 2003 US-led invasion. Abdullah, captured during the war, is held for 20 years as a prisoner of war in Iran; Tariq becomes a religious leader; and Ibrahim, badly wounded during the 1990 invasion of Kuwait, later finds work in the luxurious presidential gardens.

In the gardens, Ibrahim discovers a grisly secret – they serve as a burial ground for the regime's numerous victims. He decides to surreptitiously record every death, but when he reveals all after Saddam's fall, he becomes a target for the former regime's thugs. This brilliant, haunting novel provides an inside view of the horrors that ordinary Iraqis lived through. And although it tells a grim tale, its insidious humour and engaging narrative make it immensely enjoyable.

Ramli, an erstwhile tank commander in the army, left Iraq after his brother was hanged for being involved in an attempted coup against Saddam in 1990. He has lived in Spain since 1995. *See also: Daughter of Tigris (2019), translated by Luke Leafgren*

Frankenstein in Baghdad by Ahmed Saadawi (2013), translated by Jonathan Wright

Hadi, an alcoholic junk dealer in US-occupied Baghdad in 2005, stitches together a corpse from body parts he finds littered in the streets. He wants to convince officials that these parts should "be respected like other dead people and given a proper burial" in the war-ravaged city that is witness to sectarian killings and daily bombings. But his mosaic monster suddenly goes missing.

"Whatsitsname" – as dubbed by its creator – comes to life to avenge the deaths of the victims whose body parts it carries, so that they can rest in peace. The mission soon gets out of hand, as the composite corpse also needs to find new parts to replace putrefying old ones – and the murders across Baghdad escalate. As Whatitsname sees it: "Because I'm made up of body parts of people from diverse backgrounds – ethnicities, tribes, races and social classes – I represent the impossible mix that never was achieved in the past. I'm the first true Iraqi citizen."

Saadawi's fantastical and funny fable – which is much more than Mary Shelley's tale set in Baghdad – comes trailing superlatives and literary awards. It doesn't disappoint. A colourful cast of characters, black humour and intelligent social critique make for a superb satire on the trauma and futility of war. The Iraqi author, poet and film-maker lives in Baghdad.

The Weight of a Mustard Seed by Wendell Steavenson (2009)

General Kamel Suchet was a patriotic army officer, war hero and favourite of Saddam who eventually fell foul of the dictator's murderous regime. The general, who was once complicit in the state's atrocities, became disillusioned after Iraq's invasion of Kuwait and its subsequent retreat. Not the sort of soldier to rebel, he instead sought refuge in religion – but that didn't prevent him from being ignominiously executed as a traitor in 1999.

Steavenson, arriving in Baghdad in the wake of the 2003 Iraq war, meticulously pieces together Suchet's life by talking to his comrades-in-arms, friends and family. And through the general's waxing and waning fortunes she tracks Iraq's complex and violent recent history. By inducing an impressive array of Iraqis – both at home and in exile – to unlock their memories of Suchet and life under Saddam, Steavenson is able to present a vivid and intimate account of the era. As she tries to understand how so many ostensibly "good" men served such an evil regime, an army general explains that "all Iraqis have two or more characters. It was the only way to survive."

Steavenson, an Anglo-American journalist who reported from Iraq, tells the story, with empathy and elegance, of a prosperous nation brought low by a paranoid dictator. Her book is a valuable addition to the canon of reportage on Iraq.

Read on

A Stranger in Your Own City: Travels in the Middle East's Long War by Ghaith Abdul-Ahad (2023); The Achilles Trap: Saddam Hussein, the C.I.A., and the Origins of America's Invasion of Iraq by Steve Coll (2024); The Baghdad Clock by Shahad Al Rawi (2018), translated by Luke Leafgren; Green Zone: Imperial Life in the Emerald City by Rajiv Chandrasekaran (2006); The Corpse Washer by Sinan Antoon (2013); The Madman of Freedom Square by Hassan Blasim (2009), translated by Jonathan Wright; The Long Way Back by Fuad al-Takarli (1980), translated by Catherine Cobham

Israel

A Tale of Love and Darkness by Amos Oz (2002), translated by Nicholas de Lange

Love and darkness punctuate Oz's moving novelistic memoir. Born in Jerusalem in 1939, his coming of age coincided with Israel's own birth and early years, and he vividly evokes the city in the 1940s and 1950s, dogged by sectarian divisions and outbreaks of violence.

Oz traces his family history to eastern Europe, from where they were driven out by antisemetic nationalism to seek refuge in the Middle East. Both his parents carried their burden of disappointment: his father was a failed academic who ended up as a librarian, and his beautiful mother felt trapped in her marriage. His mother's suicide after a long depression, when Oz was just 12 years old, casts a long shadow over his remembrances. Just a couple of years after her death he rebelled against his father, leaving Jerusalem for a kibbutz, where he lived for the next 30-odd years, and changing his surname from Klausner to Oz (meaning strength or courage in Hebrew).

A clever, sensitive boy, his early infatuation with books propelled him from avid reader to writer. And this warm, witty (at times laugh-out-loud funny) bildungsroman is one of Israel's best-selling books of all time. Oz, who died in 2018, was a novelist, nonfiction writer, political activist and leading peacenik. *See also: Judas (2014); My Michael (1968), both translated by Nicholas de Lange*

To the End of the Land by David Grossman (2008), translated by Jessica Cohen

Ora is overjoyed her son Ofer is coming home after his three-year compulsory military service. But her joy turns to sorrow when he voluntarily re-enlists as yet another conflict between Israel and its enemies flares up.

Recently estranged from her husband, Ora dreads being alone at this difficult time. In a fit of magical thinking, she decides to go ahead with a hiking trip in Galilee that she and Ofer had planned, so that she won't be home if military officers come knocking on her door with bad news – and will thus somehow protect her son. She drags along her former lover and husband's best friend, Avram. A PoW who was captured and tortured by the Egyptians during the 1973 Yom Kippur war, Avram is also Ofer's biological father, though he has never seen his son.

Along the way Ora opens up to Avram about her life and about Ofer. Although the mix of monologue and flashback isn't always an easy read, Grossman manages to make the novel both epic (in its ambition) and intimate (in its narrative), painting an intriguing portrait of an anxious mother who reflects her country's insecurities.

During the writing of this book, Grossman's younger son was killed in Israel's 2006 war against Hezbollah in Lebanon.
See also: A Horse Walks Into a Bar (2017), translated by Jessica Cohen; The Yellow Wind (1988), translated by Haim Watzman

Enemies and Neighbours: Arabs and Jews in Palestine and Israel, 1917-2017 by Ian Black (2017)

In 1917, having wrested Jerusalem from the Ottoman sultan, Britain issued the fateful Balfour declaration, promising a homeland for Jews in the Holy Land. It heralded Israeli nationhood and the

1948 Nakba (catastrophe), when 750,000 Palestinians fled or were forced from their homes, never to return. The bitter and polarising conflict that the declaration unleashed continues to this day.

Through fine-grained research, a journalist's eye for detail and scrupulous impartiality Black delivers a clear and comprehensive account of the "hundred years' war" between Israelis and Palestinians. It does justice to all the seminal events, among them the 1948 Arab-Israeli war; the 1967 war that left the Arabs humiliated and the Palestinians under occupation; the two intifadas (uprisings); failed peace talks; illegal Jewish settlements; the rise of Palestinian Islamism; and Israel's lurch to the right.

Black points out that a 1947 UN resolution recommended the partition of Palestine, with 55% designated as a Jewish state. However, after the 1948 war the Palestinians were left with a mere 22%. Today even that (the West Bank and Gaza Strip) is punctured by Jewish settlements. With hopes of a two-state or binational one-state solution fast vanishing, Black depressingly concludes that no end to the conflict is in sight.

The author, who died in 2023, was a former Middle East editor at the Guardian and a visiting fellow at the London School of Economics.

Read on

Maror by Lavie Tidhar (2022); Khirbet Khizeth by S Yizhar (1978), translated by Nicholas de Lange and Yaacob Dweck; Apeirogon by Colum McCann (2020); Waking Lions by Ayelet Gundar-Goshen

(2014), translated by Sondra Silverston; All the Rivers by Dorit Rabinyan (2014), translated by Jessica Cohen; The People of Forever Are Not Afraid by Shani Boianjiu (2012); The Drive by Yair Assulin (2020), translated by Jessica Cohen

Lebanon

De Niro's Game by Rawi Hage (2006)

Set during the Lebanese civil war before and after the 1982 Israeli invasion, Hage's riveting debut novel relates the friendship and subsequent falling out between two young men. Seizing the reader from the start, the story hurtles along at an exhilarating pace.

In war-torn Beirut, with "bombs falling like monsoon rain", Bassam (the narrator) and George (AKA De Niro) are growing up in a Christian neighbourhood. The former dreams of fleeing abroad (Rome is his preferred choice), while the latter is more inclined to stay. In the violent, sectarian city electricity and water are rare commodities, guns are flourished to command respect, and corruption corrodes morality. The swaggering adolescents turn to petty crime to pay for their daily indulgences. While Bassam moves on to smuggling whisky to fund his escape, George opts for bigger game, joining a thuggish Christian militia that draws him into the bloody civil war as well as drug-fuelled crime and killing.

The spare, yet often lyrical, prose brings proximity and immediacy to this tale of brotherhood, braggadocio and, ultimately, betrayal. It's a powerful portrait of a society brutalised by war whose moral compass has been hopelessly skewed. The game of the title is Russian roulette (as played in the film The Deer Hunter).

Beirut-born Hage lived through the civil war for seven years before leaving for the US in 1982 and later emigrating to Canada. *See also: Beirut Hellfire Society (2018); Cockroach (2008)*

The Broken Mirrors/Sinalcol by Elias Khoury (2013), translated by Humphrey Davies

Karim Shammas, a young doctor, returns to Beirut in 1989, leaving behind his wife and daughters in France. The civil war he fled more than a decade earlier is still raging. What brings him back? Is it to help his brother Nasim build a hospital? Or to meet old comrades from the war? Is it nostalgia and homesickness? Or to track down a shadowy, enigmatic figure called Sinalcol, who may be his alter-ego?

To tell his story, Khoury uses the metaphor of broken mirrors to reflect and distort both past and present in war-shattered Lebanon. The swirling, looping narrative shifts back and forth in time and changes perspective – the fractured storytelling a means to mirror the destruction and displacement wrought by the interminable violence (the civil war lasted from 1975-90). "The war will never end because it's inside us," a woman tells Karim.

Khoury explores the causes of the war and the bitter schisms it created. The brothers themselves took opposing sides, with

Karim joining the leftists and Palestinians (as did Khoury) and Nasim the rightwing Christian Phalangists.

The elegantly written novel's complex structure requires perseverance, which is rewarded as the kaleidoscopic patterns become clearer. Beirut-based Khoury – novelist, playwright, journalist, activist and university lecturer – was considered a leading light of Arab literature. He died in 2024.

See also: White Masks (1992); Little Mountain (1977), both translated by Maia Tabet; Gate of the Sun (2000), translated by Humphrey Davies

Beware of Small States: Lebanon, Battleground of the Middle East by David Hirst (2010)

"If you think you understand Lebanon," goes the adage, "you haven't been properly briefed." Hirst's book challenges that received wisdom – no easy task, considering the country's tortured and tangled history. A small, fragile state in a fractious neighbourhood, Lebanon has been a battlefield for the ambitions and antagonisms of others, often resulting in proxy wars. Of the several states in the Middle East and beyond that have maltreated it, Hirst says, "none has done so more strenuously and disruptively" than Israel. And much of Lebanon's history reflects the wider Arab-Israeli conflict.

The book sweeps from the end of Ottoman rule, through European colonial domination, to the present. At independence from France in 1943, Lebanon – reflecting its fragmented religious communities, mainly Christian, Druze, Sunni and Shia – emerged with a constitution that assigned political office according to faith: a "sectarian state par excellence". The influx of tens of thousands of Palestinian refugees following the 1948 Nakba (catastrophe) further agitated communal tensions.

Over the years sectarianism has become increasingly weaponised, igniting civil wars in 1958 and 1975. With Lebanon's serial abusers Syria and Israel now joined by Iran – which armed the Shia militia Hezbollah – Hirst sees further conflict as inevitable. His detailed and well-informed account serves masterfully to enhance understanding of this complex and combustible nation. The former Guardian Middle East correspondent has lived in Beirut for more than 50 years.

Read on

An Unnecessary Woman by Rabih Alameddine (2012); Beirut Blues by Hanan al-Shaykh (1992), translated by Catherine Cobham; The Rock of Tanios by Amin Maalouf (1993), translated by Dorothy S Blair; Lebanon: A Country in Fragments by Andrew Arsan (2018); Voices of the Lost by Hoda Barakat (2020), translated by Marilyn Booth; Pity the Nation: Lebanon at War by Robert Fisk (1990/2001); The Storyteller by Pierre Jarawan (2019), translated by Sinéad Crowe and Rachel McNicholl

Libya

In the Country of Men by Hisham Matar (2006)

Matar's novel reflects the viciousness of Gaddafi's Libya through the eyes of a young boy. In Tripoli in the summer of 1979, nine-year-old Suleiman struggles to make sense of his father's disappearance and of the terror it induces in the adults around him. And that's not all the boy has to deal with. Why is his mother becoming increasingly dependent on the illicit "medicine" supplied by the baker; why is she burning the books his father loves; why is the man in the car outside his house always asking him for the names of his father's friends; and why is his best friend's father on television begging for his life before being hanged?

In this country of torturers and their victims, boys must be men – but these concerns weigh heavily on Suleiman and leave him permanently on edge. He finds himself in a state of "quiet panic, as if at any moment the rug could be pulled from beneath my feet".

Matar distills his own experiences into this emotionally wrenching novel of love, repression and betrayal. His father disappeared into Gaddafi's jails in 1990, and his whereabouts remain unknown. In the Country of Men, Matar's debut novel, was shortlisted for the Man Booker prize. The author lives in the UK. *See also: The Return: Fathers, Sons and the Land In Between (2016), My Friends (2023)*

The Bleeding of the Stone by Ibrahim al-Koni (2002), translated by May Jayyusi and Christopher Tingley

Koni's magic realism mixes reality, fantasy and mysticism to relate this ecological fable, set in the desert of southern Libya. Asouf, a vegetarian Bedouin goatherd who lives alone, reveres the delicate balance between man and nature in that harsh environment. He holds the key to some of the region's secrets, being custodian of the ancient paintings on the walls of the wadi and the only person who knows the whereabouts of the legendary waddan, a wild mountain sheep famed for its meat.

He shuns contact with his fellow man, interacting only with the occasional passing caravan. But both he and the waddan, which he holds to be sacred, come under threat with the arrival of two hunters who have a craving for meat. The men have already slaughtered the herds of gazelle that roamed the desert and now have their hearts set on eating waddan meat. They demand that Asouf reveal the sheeps' hiding place.

Tradition and greed clash head on in a tale replete with aphorisms and poetic turns of phrase. It offers a very different view of the Arab world from that which is generally portrayed.

Koni is a Libyan Tuareg writer whose work reflects his desert origins.

See also: Gold Dust (1990), translated by Elliott Colla

Sandstorm: Libya from Gaddafi to Revolution by Lindsey Hilsum (2012)

In this admirable account of Gaddafi's downfall, Hilsum reports first-hand on the 2011 uprising against the Libyan leader but sets it against a backdrop of the country's history. We follow the colonel's fortunes from young, charismatic, revolutionary army officer to bizarre, Botoxed, delusional dictator.

In the west, the Arab world's longest-ruling strongman – in power for 42 years – was seen as a vile, narcissistic buffoon; a top arms supplier to terrorist and rebel groups worldwide; and an architect of the Lockerbie bombing. In Libya, Gaddafi cowed the population, silencing dissent with "disappearances", torture and public hangings; disseminated his weird and wacky ideas through the ubiquitous Green Book; and allowed his family to plunder state assets (mostly the billions of dollars earned from oil sales).

The west flip-flopped over relations – he was sometimes pariah, sometimes friend – but finally used Nato planes to help topple him. The seeds of Gaddafi's eventual fall were sown in 1996 following a massacre at Tripoli's Abu Salim jail, when around 1,300 political prisoners were gunned down. It was a wound that never healed for the families of the murdered men, and their protests sparked the rebellion in Benghazi that led to the so-called Brother Leader's bloody denouement.

Hilsum, international editor for Channel 4 News, has written a perceptive and very readable book that is an excellent primer on Libya.

Read On

The Burning Shores: Inside the Battle for the New Libya by Frederic Wehrey (2018); Under the Tripoli Sky by Kamal Ben Hameda (2014), translated by Adriana Hunter; The Dictator's Last Night by Yasmina Khadra (2015), translated by Julian Evans

Morocco

The Last Friend by Tahar Ben Jelloun (2004), translated by Kevin Michel Capé and Hazel Rowley

Teenagers Ali and Mamed (Mohammed) meet at a French lycée in Tangiers at the end of the 1950s in newly independent Morocco. Although very different characters, they form an intense friendship that lasts around 40 years. As adolescents, they discover – and pursue – sex and politics. Their friendship endures through the decades of Morocco's turbulent post-colonial history, with King Hassan II's autocratic reign and the independence war in neighbouring Algeria providing a backdrop. Arrested during student protests in 1966, imprisoned and then detained in a military boot camp for 18 months (echoing Jelloun's own experience), the harshness of what they went through serves to strengthen their bond.

As they later settle into more conventional lives – with wives, children and jobs – they maintain their friendship, despite their spouses being jealous of their closeness and Mamed emigrating to Sweden. But a sudden and surprising act of betrayal finally ruptures their alliance. The story is told first in Ali's voice, then in Mamed's, and finally Ramon, a mutual friend, offers a foot-note. This heartfelt treatise on the complex nature of friendship is elegantly crafted, and the two friends' coming-of-age tale reflects the story of Morocco's post-independence generation.

Ben Jelloun, an award-winning novelist, poet and essayist, was born in Fez but went into self-imposed exile in France in 1971, aged 27.

See also: This Blinding Absence of Light (2000), translated by Linda Coverdale; Corruption (1994), translated by Carol Volk

Secret Son by Laila Lalami (2009)

Yousef lives in a Casablanca slum with his struggling, "widowed" mother. The 19-year-old, who attends university on a scholarship, feels burdened by the indignity of being both poor and fatherless, and longs for a better life. He is shocked one day to discover that not only is his father alive, he's also a rich businessman, Nabil Amrani, who lives across town. Yousef goes to see him, and Amrani – who has recently fallen out with his daughter – surpris-ingly, welcomes his "secret son", providing him with a penthouse flat and a job.

Yousef is happy to join the "Mercedes-and-Marlboro" clique, and turns his back on his mother and his slum-dwelling friends. But his fall from grace is as rapid as his rise, and he is suddenly cast out by the Amrani clan. On returning to his old home, Yousef finds that Islamic fundamentalists have built their headquarters in the slum and insinuated themselves into the lives of disaffected youngsters. Angry and disillusioned, he is swept up in their plans.

Lalami's powerful page-turner, her debut novel, deftly portrays the simmering tensions of class, corruption, politics and religion in contemporary Moroccan society. The author, born and raised in Morocco, now lives in Los Angeles. "In Morocco," she says, "a lot of what determines your power in society is class and who your family knows."

See also: Hope and Other Dangerous Pursuits (2005)

Morocco: The Islamist Awakening and Other Challenges by Marvine Howe (2005)

Since independence in 1956 from its colonial masters France and Spain, Morocco has presented itself as a stable, moderate Muslim country on the road to democracy. But behind that facade lies an "Islamic-based authoritarian monarchy, endowed with a pervasive security system". Howe uses her many personal contacts and interviews with key players to offer a clear and candid assessment of the country, focusing on its recent history and politics.

King Hassan II's despotic reign (1961-99), which included the "years of lead" in the 1970s and 1980s – a period of fierce repression – still casts a long shadow. And the bombings in Casablanca in 2003 and Madrid in 2004 – blamed mainly on Moroccans – brought into sharp focus Islamist extremism. These events called into question the belief in Moroccan exceptionalism. Hopes that Mohammed VI, who succeeded his father in 1999, would usher in change have not been realised as he has been unwilling to relinquish his absolute control over the levers of state and religion.

Howe is banking on civil society – a relatively free press and more than 30,000 associations – to tackle the challenges of democratisation, religious extremism, women's rights, corruption and inequality. "Moroccans are clamouring for justice, accountability and hope," she says. "And they want change now." Howe, a former New York Times journalist, has a long association with Morocco.

Read on

The Country of Others by Leila Slimani (2020), tranlated by Sam Taylor; Heirs to the Past by Driss Chraïbi (1962), translated by Len Ortzen; The Spider's House by Paul Bowles (1955); For Bread Alone by Mohamed Choukri (1972), translated by Paul Bowles; Horses of God by Mahi Binebine (2010), translated by Lulu Norman; Arabian Nights: In Search of Morocco, Through Its Stories and Storytellers by Tahir Shah (2008); The Arch and the Butterfly by Mohammed Achaari (2010), translated by Aida Bamia; Lords of the Atlas by

Gavin Maxwell (1966); The Boy Who Set the Fire & Other Stories by Mohammed Mrabet (1975), translated by Paul Bowles

Palestine

Mornings in Jenin by Susan Abulhawa (2006)

Heart-wrenching, haunting and highly readable, Abulhawa's novel tells the story of a Palestinian family driven from their village in the 1948 war with Israel. Amal, the granddaughter of the patriarch, narrates her family's turbulent tale of expulsion and exile over four generations as the refugees struggle against "being erased from the world".

On their way to a camp in Jenin, on the West Bank, Amal's older brother is snatched by an Israeli soldier as a son for his barren wife – and brought up as a Jew, to become an implacable foe of the Arabs. Her younger brother, meanwhile, joins the fedayeen to fight against Israel, sacrificing everything in the struggle for Palestine. The tragedy deepens when, in the 1967 six-day war, Amal is injured, her father is killed and her mother suffers a mental breakdown. The peripatetic Amal, for whom Palestine is a home she never knew, eventually finds herself in exile alone in the US.

This is an unmistakably political novel whose luminous prose fizzes with passion and pique. And by intertwining her fictitious tale with historical events and figures, Abulhawa's story of one family from an obscure village "for ever trapped by longing" gives voice to the tragedy of the Palestinian people.

The author, born to Palestinian refugees of the 1967 war, lives in the US.

See also: The Blue Between Sky and Water (2015); Against the Loveless World (2020)

Enter Ghost by Isabella Hammad (2023)

Hammad's sharply observed and emotionally absorbing novel, set in present-day Palestine and Israel, uses a subtle marriage of the personal and the political to deal with love, loss, identity and belonging.

Sonia Nasir, a British-Palestinian stage actor, returns to her homeland after many years to reconnect with her sister Haneen and with her roots, and to escape a failed love affair in London. Although she's hoping to take a break from acting, Sonia is roped into playing Gertude in an Arabic version of Hamlet in the West Bank directed by her sister's friend, the idealistic Mariam.

Reluctant to start with, Sonia soon falls in with the troupe as the struggle to overcome obstacles put in their way gives her a sense of belonging. Under the dark shadow of the occupation, putting on the play is no easy task. The actors face daily humiliations by Israeli soldiers at checkpoints, interrogations, detentions, being spied on and funding problems, all against a backdrop of political tumult and violence. But seeing the play through is an act of defiance, and Mariam is determined to press on. She tells Sonia: "If we let disaster stand in our way, we will never do anything. Every day here is a disaster." For Palestinians, something is certainly rotten in the state of Israel.

Hammad, a British-Palestinian, wears her politics on her sleeve and says her relationship with Palestine is "complex, intellectual and emotional".

See also: The Parisienne (2019); Recognising the Stranger: On Palestine and Narrative (2024)

Enemies and Neighbours: Arabs and Jews in Palestine and Israel, 1917-2017 by Ian Black (2017)

In 1917, having wrested Jerusalem from the Ottoman sultan, Britain issued the fateful Balfour declaration, promising a homeland for Jews in the Holy Land. It heralded Israeli nationhood and the 1948 Nakba (catastrophe), when 750,000 Palestinians fled or were forced from their homes, never to return. The bitter and polarising conflict that the declaration unleashed continues to this day.

Through fine-grained research, a journalist's eye for detail and scrupulous impartiality Black delivers a clear and comprehensive account of the "hundred years' war" between Israelis and Palestinians. It does justice to all the seminal events, among them: the 1948 Arab-Israeli war; the 1967 war that left the Arabs humiliated and the Palestinians under occupation; the two intifadas (uprisings); failed peace talks; illegal Jewish settlements; the rise of Palestinian Islamism; and Israel's lurch to the right.

Black points out that a 1947 UN resolution recommended the partition of Palestine, with 55% designated as a Jewish state. However, after the 1948 war the Palestinians were left with a mere 22%. Today even that (the West Bank and Gaza Strip) is punctured by Jewish settlements. With hopes of a two-state or binational one-state solution fast vanishing, Black depressingly concludes that no end to the conflict is in sight.

The author, who died in 2023, was a former Middle East editor at the Guardian and a visiting fellow at the London School of Economics.

Read on

A Day in the Life of Abed Salama: A Palestine Story by Nathan Thrall (2023); The Hundred Years' War on Palestine: A History of Colonial Conquest and Resistance by Rashid Khalidi (2020); Minor Detail by Adania Shibli (2017), translated by Elisabeth Jacquette; The Question of Palestine by Edward Said (1979); Apeirogon by Colum McCann (2020); Salt Houses by Hala Alyan (2017); Men in the Sun and Other Palestinian Stories by Ghassan Kanafani (1962), translated by Hilary Kilpatrick; The Way to the Spring: Life and Death in Palestine by Ben Ehrenreich (2016); Gate of the Sun by Elias Khoury (2000), translated by Humphrey Davies; The Book of Disappearance by Ibtisam Azem (2014), translated by Sinan Antoon

Saudi Arabia

Cities of Salt by Abdelrahman Munif (1984), translated by Peter Theroux

Munif's sprawling novel chronicles the cultural clash between the Orient and the Occident that ensues after oil is discovered by Americans in a poor Bedouin desert community. The residents of an oasis village in an unnamed Gulf kingdom – a thinly veiled Saudi Arabia – find their traditional way of life upended when the foreigners start drilling and effectively colonise the region in the 1930s.

The two communities live in separate towns as the Americans arrogate to themselves the best housing and facilities, relegating their Arab workers to harsher living and working conditions. Munif introduces a large cast of characters (at times it's hard to keep track of them) as he tells the story through the eyes of the Arab protagonists, who find themselves caught up in the storm of upheaval, rivalries and corruption. The story gathers momentum as their dissatisfaction grows.

This avowedly political novel, the first in a trilogy, is infused with humour, elegant prose and passion. Although regarded as a classic of modern Arab literature, it was banned in several Middle East countries – including Munif's native Saudi Arabia. The author, an oil industry insider and political activist, was stripped of his Saudi citizenship for his dissidence. He died in Damascus in 2004.

See also: *The Trench* (1991); *Variations on Night and Day* (1993), both translated by Peter Theroux

Girls of Riyadh by Rajaa Alsanea (2005), translated by Rajaa Alsanea and Mary Booth

This Saudi version of Sex and the City caused a furore on publication in Arabic and was – inevitably – banned in its home country, propelling it to bestseller status in the Middle East and translation into English. Girls of Riyadh charts the (fictional) lives of four twentysomething friends in the Saudi capital as they fall in and out of love in pursuit of suitable husbands. It's written as a series of weekly emails, "revealing new and thrilling developments", sent out by one of their sassy girlfriends, who remains anonymous. Alsanea boldly tackles a number of taboos, exposing the fault lines in a patriarchal society "riddled with hypocrisy and drugged by contradictions". Sadeem, Gamrah, Lamees and Michelle (the last is half Saudi, half American) are from the privileged "velvet class". Though burqa-clad in public and seemingly adhering to the severe Saudi traditions, they clandestinely date, drink, drive and have plastic surgery (banned under Islamic law). Men – too often sexist and controlling – come off badly in this tale, in which women pay a high price for failed relationships, finding themselves sidelined and stigmatised.

This witty and engaging novel offers a rare glimpse into a slice of life behind the veil as the "girls" of Riyadh kick back against the kingdom's ultra-conservative social mores. The author is a Saudi endodontist, and this is her debut novel.

MBS: The Rise to Power of Mohammed bin Salman by Ben Hubbard (2020)

Hubbard's well-informed and well-sourced account compellingly charts the rise of the ruthless young crown prince, a divisive figure who is now Saudi Arabia's de facto ruler. Once an outlier in the running for the crown, the machiavellian Mohammed bin Salman (known as MBS) plotted his way up the chain of succession, declaring himself winner in the game of thrones. He is now remaking the country in his image.

When his father Salman became king in 2015, MBS, the favourite son, took charge of defence, the economy, religion and oil. The new crown prince certainly shook things up in the sclerotic kingdom. Although something of a reformer – looking to diversify the economy and easing restrictions on music, film and female drivers – he has revealed himself to be an autocrat who cracks down harshly on dissent and crushes his enemies.

Events that have unfolded on the crown prince's watch include intervening militarily in neighbouring Yemen's civil war; the (in)famous "sheikhdown" that saw hundreds of rich and powerful family members and businessmen detained in Riyadh's Ritz Carlton Hotel, ostensibly in a crackdown on corruption; a palace coup to oust his cousin Mohammed bin Nayef, the erstwhile crown prince; and the savage murder of the dissident journalist Jamal Khashoggi.

Hubbard, an Arabic-speaking American journalist, spent nearly 15 years in the Middle East reporting for the New York Times.

Read on

Inside the Kingdom: Kings, Clerics, Modernists, Terrorists and the Struggle for Saudi Arabia by Robert Lacey (2009); Engulfed: How Saudi Arabia Bought Sport, and the World by James Montague (2025); Blood and Oil: Mohammed bin Salman's Ruthless Quest for Global Power by Bradley Hope and Justin Scheck; Adama by Turki al-Hamad (2003), translated by Robin Bray; Throwing Sparks by Abdo Khal (2010), translated by Maia Tabet and Michael K Scott; The Ruins of Us by Keija Parssinen (2012); The Consequences of Love by Sulaiman Addonia (2008)

Syria

The Dark Side of Love by Rafik Schami (2004), translated by Anthea Bell

Schami's monumental novel of forbidden love is an opulent, intricately assembled mosaic of stories. With its myriad digressions and vast array of characters, it isn't always an easy read – but persistence is richly rewarded. At its heart is the Romeo and Juliet-like romance between Farid Mushtak and Rana Shahid, whose Christian clans – one Catholic, the other Greek Orthodox – have been engaged in a blood feud over generations. Originally from the mountain village of Mala, the rival families later take their enmity to Damascus, which is vividly and lovingly portrayed.

The compelling tale of the star-crossed couple straddles love, lust, betrayal and revenge, while laying bare the sins of a male-dominated society. It sweeps through much of Syria's turbulent 20th-century history as the country endures French occupation, military coups, union with Egypt and war with Israel.

Schami illuminates the dark side not just of love, but also of religion and politics. The last, frequently blighted by violence and repression, causes Farid to pay dearly for his radical affiliations. "Knowledge is a lock," says one character, "and the key to it is a question, but we're not allowed to ask questions in this country."

The author, who fled Syria in 1970 and now lives in Germany, says the catalyst for the novel was witnessing an "honour killing" on the streets of Damascus in 1962.

See also: The Calligrapher's Secret (2008), translated by Anthea Bell; Sophia: Or the Beginning of All Tales (2018), translated by Monique Arav and John Hannon

In Praise of Hatred by Khaled Khalifa (2012), translated by Leri Price

This multi-layered novel explores the rise of religious extremism in Syria from a female perspective. It's set in the early 1980s, during the bloody struggle between the Muslim Brotherhood and the ostensibly secular regime of Hafez al-Assad (Bashar's father), in which thousands died.

The unnamed narrator, a young girl growing up in her grand-parents' house in Aleppo with her three aunts, finds her cloistered existence encroached upon by the tumultuous events taking place in the country. Under the influence of an uncle, she becomes increasingly conservative and religious, finally embracing fanat-icism and declaring herself a *mujahida*, a Muslim warrior. She becomes enthused by sectarian animosity, believing that "we need hatred to give our lives meaning". As the conflict esca-lates, and "bodies on both sides fall like ripened berries", family members are caught up in the battle and the ferocious repression that follows. She is eventually jailed and tortured for her links to the Islamists. During her long, harsh spell in prison she realises "hatred [is] worthy of praise as it lives within us exactly as love does". That hatred has echoes in the country's civil war today.

Khalifa's book was banned in Syria. Despite his run-ins with the Assad regime, the author – also a well-known screenwriter – continued to live in Damascus until his death in 2023.
See also: No Knives in the Kitchens of This City: A Novel (2013); Death Is Hard Work (2016), No One Prayed Over Their Graves (2023), all translated by Leri Price

Burning Country: Syrians in Revolution and War by Robin Yassin-Kassab and Leila al-Shami (2016)

Burning Country meshes first-hand testimonies with lucid analysis to chronicle the 2011 Syrian revolution from the grassroots up. It is a people's history, giving voice to the ordinary citizens who defied the Assad "realm of fear".

The early chapters provide historical context, charting how the minority Shia Alawite sect – to which the Assad family belongs – went from society's margins to its mainstream, seizing power in the 1960s. Hafez al-Assad's dictatorship presented a facade of socialism and secularism behind which lurked crony capitalism and sectarianism. Bashar's takeover after his father's death in 2000 brought hopes of reform, which remained unfulfilled. When peaceful protesters took to the streets in 2011, the regime's response was savage. After that "baptism of horror", the revolt became fiercer. It militarised, split into factions, and an increasing number of the fighters were Islamist.

In the denouement that followed, the country became the site "of proxy wars, of Sunni-Shia rivalries, of foreign interventions". And it brought the biggest refugee crisis since the second world war. The authors lament the international community's failure to support the moderate opposition movements and to prevent the country's fragmentation and mutilation.

Intelligent, indignant and hugely empathetic, Burning Country tells us much of what we need to know about Syria. Yassin-Kassab and Al-Shami are British-Syrians, the former a commentator and novelist, the latter an activist.

Read on

Assad or We Burn the Country by Sam Dagher (2019); The Silence and the Roar by Nihad Sirees (2013), translated by Max Weiss; The Beekeeper of Aleppo by Christy Lefteri (2019); The Unexpected Love Objects of Dunya Noor by Rana Haddad (2018); Sabriya: Damascus Bitter Sweet by Ulfat Idlibi (1995), translated by Peter Clark; The Frightened Ones by Dima Wannous (2017), translated by Elisabeth Jaquette

Yemen

A Land Without Jasmine by Wajdi al-Ahdal (2012), translated by William Maynard Hutchins

When beautiful, virtuous Jasmine suddenly disappears without a trace, it sets heads shaking and tongues wagging. Has the young university student run away, or has she been raped and murdered? Those who knew her seem keen to rush to judgment, without knowing what really happened.

Set in the bustling city of Sana'a, the novella paints an unflinching picture of the challenges faced by women in a patriarchal and sexually repressed society. Although fully veiled, Jasmine is subjected to what she calls "a noxious type of male violence" – men looking lustfully at her. "This gaze by repressed males assaults my skin … [and] makes my blood boil."

When Inspector Abdurrabbih Ubayd al-Adini takes charge of Jasmine's case, he finds boundless motives and suspects for her vanishing. Meanwhile, armed men from her tribe – "for whom a daughter's honour is the red line; any creature crossing that line is destined to die" – have gathered at her home, piling pressure on the policeman.

This short work gives voice to six protagonists, including Jasmine, who have different takes on the events that unfold. The tactile prose and thriller-like story offers a window into Yemen's social complexities and contradictions.

Al-Ahdal, a Yemeni author and playwright, continues to be provocative. He was forced into exile for a number of years after the publication of his controversial debut novel, Mountain Boats, in 2002.

They Die Strangers: A Novella and Stories From Yemen by Mohammad Abdul-Wali (1971), translated by Abubaker Bagader and Deborah Akers

Together, these stories offer a poignant reflection on displacement – a look into the lives of Yemenis forced by war and poverty to flee their homeland in the 1950s and 1960s. Foreigners both at home and abroad, they grapple with loss and longing, and struggle to fit into their new surroundings, their outlook clouded by bitterness and nostalgia.

In the novella, a Yemeni shopkeeper in the Ethiopian capital, Addis Ababa, although successful and popular, yearns for his homeland and for his wife and son. He sends almost all his money home and dreams of returning as a rich man to be revered by the local townspeople. In simple, sparse prose, the writer empathetically conveys the difficulties and dilemmas of emigre lives.

Abdul-Wali, regarded as a leading light of Yemeni fiction, was born in Ethiopia to a Yemeni father and an Ethiopian mother. He led a peripatetic and eventful life. Expelled from Egypt for his radical politics and from East Germany for alleged spying, he faced censorship from Muslim leaders in Yemen for his writing, and spent time in jail after falling out with the Yemeni government. In Ethiopia he was regarded as a *muwallad* (person of mixed blood) and was sensitive to racism, a subject often present in his stories. He died in a plane crash in 1973, aged 33.

Yemen: What Everyone Needs to Know by Asher Orkaby (2020)

"Ruling Yemen is like dancing on the heads of snakes," according to Ali Abdullah Saleh. The machiavellian former military man should know; he ruled for 33 years. His autocratic regime finally succumbed to the Arab spring protests in 2011, but he continued to play a role in events until he was killed in 2017 during the civil war. Yemen: What Everyone Needs to Know serves as a short, sharp, accessible primer on this enigmatic nation – the poorest Arab state, often overlooked – that has recently been vaulted into the news.

Split between the Ottoman Empire (north) and Britain (Aden, in the south) the two Yemeni entities gained independence as separate nations, in 1918 and 1967 respectively. Following a troubled history that saw transitions through a kingdom, a republic and a communist state, north and south finally unified as the Republic of Yemen in 1990. But it brought no end to the turbulence, with civil and secessionist wars, border disputes with Saudi Arabia, jihadi terrorist attacks, and uprisings.

The latest, ongoing, insurgency by the Houthis – a religious revivalist movement that became a major military and political force – which began in 2014, has metastasised into a long-running civil war. Fuelled by foreign intervention, with a Saudi-led coalition and the west backing the internationally recognised government and Iran supporting the insurgents, the conflict has triggered a desperate humanitarian crisis, bringing the prospect of famine.

Orkaby is a research associate and lecturer at Harvard University. *See also: Beyond the Arab Cold War: The International History of the Yemen Civil War, 1962-68 (2017)*

Read on

What Have You Left Behind?: Voices From a Forgotten War by Bushra al-Maqtari (2022), translated by Sawad Hussain; Henna

House by Nomi Eve (2014); Yemen: Travels in Dictionary Land by Tim Mackintosh-Smith (1997); Yemen in Crisis: Devastating Conflict, Fragile Hope by Helen Lackner (2017); The Hostage by Zayd Mutee' Dammaj (1994), translated by May Jayyusi and Christopher Tingley

Middle East and North Africa general

Black Wave: Saudi Arabia, Iran and the Rivalry That Unravelled the Middle East by Kim Ghattas (2020)

The Lebanese journalist and former BBC correspondent explores how the friction between Saudi Arabia and Iran, ignited by the 1979 Iranian Revolution, has shaped Middle Eastern politics and fuelled Sunni-Shia sectarianism across the region.

A Line in the Sand: Britain, France and the Struggle That Shaped the Middle East by James Barr (2009)

A lucid, richly detailed telling of the sordid efforts by Britain and France to carve up the region in the wake of the Ottoman empire's collapse – the consequences of which resonate to this day.

See also: Lords of the Desert (2018)

The Arabs: A History by Eugene Rogan (2018)

An excellent overview of Arab history, from the Ottoman empire to the present day, that sweeps across countries from north Africa to west Asia.

See also: The Damascus Events: The 1860 Massacre and the Destruction of the Old Ottoman World (2024)

Read on

Battleground: Ten Conflicts That Explain the New Middle East by Christopher Phillips (2024); The Making of the Modern Middle East: A Personal History by Jeremy Bowen (2022); The House Divided: Sunni, Shia and the Making of the Middle East by Barnaby Rogerson (2024)

Asia

Afghanistan

The Kite Runner by Khaled Hosseini (2003)

Hosseini's remarkable and wildly successful debut novel vividly captures the colour and complexities of modern Afghanistan. His engaging coming-of-age story, set against the country's recent history, is an epic tale of love, betrayal, exile – and redemption.

Amir's childhood playmate, Hassan, is the son of a servant, as well as a being friend. The two motherless boys were nursed by the same woman on orders from Amir's father. In reality, however, a gulf divides the privileged Amir, a Pashtun and a Sunni, and Hassan, who is from the despised Hazara minority and a Shia. The boys, who have a passion for kites, win Kabul's annual kite-flying competition. But their victory is soured by Amir's cowardice and betrayal of Hassan.

Following the king's overthrow in 1973, war rumbles across Afghanistan as the country – along with Amir's childhood certainties – begins to unravel. After the Russians invade, Amir and his father escape to Pakistan and seek asylum in the US. Amir's guilt over Hassan torments him in exile. He sees a chance to redeem himself when a letter arrives from a family friend in Pakistan telling him "there's a way to be good again". But it means he must return to a repressive and dangerous Taliban-ruled Afghanistan.

Hosseini's family was granted political asylum in the US following the Russian invasion of Afghanistan in 1979. He qualified as a doctor before becoming a best-selling author.

See also: A Thousand Splendid Suns (2007); And the Mountains Echoed (2013)

The Patience Stone by Atiq Rahimi (2008), translated by Polly McLean

In a bare room in a war zone, a woman nurses her comatose husband, who has a bullet lodged in his neck. The jihadist fighter was injured in a spat about honour rather than in battle. The nameless woman has been abandoned by her family and left to care for him and two young daughters alone. The fighting taking place outside – gunfire, explosions and screams – noisily intrudes from time to time.

While tending to her husband, the woman begins to reveal grievances and confide long-buried secrets to the unconscious man. Emboldened by his silence, her outpourings become ever more shocking as she rails against men, war, marriage and even God. The wounded husband becomes her patience stone of Persian legend: a magical stone to which "you confess everything [that] you don't dare tell anyone". It absorbs all secrets, until one day it explodes and sets the confessor free from torment.

Rahimi's haunting, beautifully written and extraordinarily powerful tale lifts the veil on the harsh lives of Afghan women. The novelist and film-maker fled Afghanistan during the Soviet occupation and sought asylum in France. For this, his fourth, novel, he chose to write in French over his native Dari. It won the Prix Goncourt, France's top literary prize.

See also: Earth and Ashes (1999), translated by Erdag M Goknar; A Thousand Rooms of Dreams and Fear (2002), translated by Sarah Maguire and Yama Yari

Butcher & Bolt: Two Hundred Years of Foreign Engagement in Afghanistan by David Loyn (2008)

In Afghanistan – the land it is said no outsider can conquer – history keeps repeating itself as foreign invaders stubbornly refuse to learn from the past. Loyn chronicles 200 years of disastrous outside interference, beginning in 1809: first by the British, then by the Russians and, most recently, by the Americans. Whether for politics or profit, all try to pacify the country and meddle in its affairs – and all pay dearly in blood and treasure.

The British, unable to subdue Afghanistan, gain a reputation for vengeful forays into the country to butcher local tribesmen and then bolt. Loyn draws parallels between past adventures and the recent western entanglement – regime change, calls for jihad – and is scathing about foreigners' refusal to understand Afghan society and politics. "The US discovered, as Britain and Russia had before, that taking Afghanistan was the easy bit," he writes. Any subsequent plans are inevitably frustrated.

After driving out the Taliban in 2001, the US-backed regime allowed massive corruption to set in and failed to deliver justice or fair policing. As a result, within five years, the Taliban re-emerged. Loyn, writing before the disastrous US pullout, advocates talks as the only solution to ending the conflict. His journalist's eye and writing style, together with an expert marshalling of facts, deliver an exemplary history lesson. The long-time BBC foreign correspondent has reported extensively from Afghanistan.

See also: The Long War: The Inside Story of America and Afghanistan Since 9/11 (2021)

Read on

The Wasted Vigil by Nadeem Aslam (2008); Farewell Kabul: From Afghanistan to a More Dangerous World by Christina Lamb (2015); The Afghans: Three Lives Through War, Love and Revolt by Åsne Seierstad (2024), translated by Sean Kinsella; Dear Zari: Hidden Stories from Women of Afghanistan by Zarghuna Kargar (2011); The Pearl that Broke Its Shell by Nadia Hashimi (2014); Return of a King: The Battle for Afghanistan by William Dalrymple (2012); A Fort of Nine Towers by Qais Akbar Omar (2013); The Swallows Of Kabul by Yasmina Khadra (2002), translated by John Cullen; My Dear Kabul: A Year in the Life of an Afghan Women's Writing Group (2024)

Bangladesh

A Golden Age by Tahmima Anam (2007)

Anam's strikingly assured debut novel, set amid Bangladesh's bloody birth pangs, features a pulsing, page-turning narrative. It's 1971, and Bengali secessionist stirrings in East Pakistan – separated from West Pakistan by more than 1,000 miles of India – are gathering pace. Following a savage crackdown by the Pakistani army, the tensions explode into war. In Dhaka, the regional capital, Rehana Haque, a widow, and her two children – Sohail, 19, and Maya, 17 – are caught up in the maelstrom, and the independence struggle is reflected through their eyes.

Rehana is desperate to protect her children and keep the family together, remembering a time "when their faces were fresh, unmarked by grief or history". Initially ambivalent about the revolutionary cause, she is drawn in by Sohail and Maya, who commit to it totally as guerrilla fighter and propagandist respectively. Their mother is soon helping to shield wounded combatants and conceal arms caches, proving herself to be both daring and discreet.

The finely wrought characters, taut and beautifully evocative prose, and undercurrent of foreboding make for an enthralling read. A Golden Age, the first book in Anam's Bengal trilogy, is richly rendered historical fiction. The seed of the novel was her grandmother's true story of her house being raided by the Pakistani army in a search for weapons during the war. The Dhaka-born author lives in London.

See also: The Good Muslim (2011); The Bones of Grace (2016)

Scenes From Early Life by Philip Hensher (2012)

Hensher's fictionalised memoir is based on the life of his Bangladeshi husband. It's narrated by Saadi, a boy born into an upper middle-class Bengali family in late 1970, just months before East Pakistan is plunged into an ugly civil war from which it emerges as Bangladesh.

The clampdown on Bengali language and culture by the Pakistani authorities (Saadi's grandfather walls up his precious books in the basement awaiting better times) and the civil war that follows mark a turbulent interregnum. The family survives, as "the violence and terror washed up against the gate of the house, but no further".

Growing up during the new nation's struggle and independence, Saadi recounts his idyllic childhood at his grandfather's mansion in a posh Dacca (later Dhaka) neighbourhood. He is surrounded by an extended family of siblings, parents, grandparents, uncles and aunts, along with household employees, friends and neighbours – among whom is Sheikh Mujib, Bangladesh's first leader.

Hensher flawlessly weaves together social and political events, relationships, cultural mores and quotidian domestic life. His affectionate and humorous storytelling – in a warm glow of nostalgia – is immensely endearing. The vividly drawn portrait of a family in the 1970s, through finely crafted vignettes, provides an insight into a country less travelled by westerners.

The British novelist and critic lives in London and Geneva.
See also: The Mulberry Empire (2002)

A History of Bangladesh by Willem van Schendel (2009/2020)

Bangladesh as an independent country has only existed since 1971, but Van Schendel takes a long view – covering social, economic and political history across two millennia in the "Bengal delta", the region that mutated into the Bengali nation. It has been a painful, often bloody, transition from being part of Bengal in India to East Bengal to East Pakistan and finally to Bangladesh.

Van Schendel telescopes pre-history into the first chapter, and then chronologically traverses the long colonial periods (Mughal and British); the failed experiment as East Pakistan after the partition of India in 1947; armed conflict with Pakistan that led to secession in 1971; and finally key developments in Bangladesh up to the present day.

The nasty nine-month independence war ended when Indian troops crossed the border and backed the insurgents. Fifty years on, the war is still a "political juggernaut", its memory manipulated and exploited in power struggles today. The new nation has mirrored some of the behaviour of its former Pakistani foe, including corruption, coups, a chequered democracy and the creeping Islamisation of politics. The author, however, signals optimism, praising people's "upbeat resilience that is one of the region's most valuable historical legacies".

Van Schendel's lively, informative overview makes a valuable contribution to better understanding this vibrant nation. The Dutch historian lectured on Asia at the University of Amsterdam.

Read on

The Blood Telegram: Nixon, Kissinger and a Forgotten Genocide by Gary J Bass (2013); The Storm by Arif Anwar (2018); Galpa: Short Stories by Bangladeshi Women (2015), edited by Niaz Zaman and Firdous Azim; Brick Lane by Monica Ali (2003)

Cambodia

In the Shadow of the Banyan by Vaddey Ratner (2012)

In 1975, the murderous Khmer Rouge triumphed in Cambodia's civil war and sought to take the country "all the way back to nothing", as a character in Ratner's searing autobiographical novel puts it. The story is told through the eyes of seven-year-old Raami, of royal lineage, who bears witness to the country's descent into misery. Her cosseted childhood is cruelly ended when soldiers force her family out of their home in Phnom Penh to join the exodus of people expelled from the cities into the countryside in the regime's pursuit of an agrarian, Maoist paradise.

It's a tale of gut-wrenching hardship and despair, as Raami and her family are forced into hard labour and moved from village to village. Close family members, including her beloved father, succumb to starvation, disease and summary execution. Up to 2 million people – about a quarter of Cambodia's population – died during the Khmer Rouge's four-year reign of terror. Despite its grim storyline, this novel of compelling power is also a paean to hope, love and the resilience of the human spirit.

"Raami's story is essentially my own," says the author, who was five years old when the Khmer Rouge seized power. She and her mother fled Cambodia in 1979 after the fall of the regime, and Ratner arrived in the US as a refugee in 1981.
See also: Music of the Ghosts (2017)

The King's Last Song by Geoff Ryman (2006)

In a dig near the Angkor Wat temples in 2004, archaeologists discover the 12th-century memoirs of Cambodia's most powerful king etched on gold leaves to avoid decay. They realise that secrecy is of the essence as bitterly divided factions harking back to the Khmer Rouge era would seek to possess the valuable trove for their own ends. But despite their best efforts, word gets out. The treasure is stolen and the Frenchman leading the UN project, Luc Andrade, is kidnapped by a group still loyal to the Khmer Rouge, and his life put in grave danger.

Ryman's richly textured novel tells two deftly interwoven stories, set some 800 years apart, as it flashes back and forth between the life of Jayavarman VII and turbulent, modern-day Cambodia. Two Cambodians – a hardened and cynical ex-Khmer Rouge soldier and a young motoboy (motorcycle taxi driver) whose parents were killed by Pol Pot's regime – join forces to recover the gold leaves and rescue their captive mentor. However, the uninterred animosities and unresolved conflicts of the country's recent past threaten their mission – and their relationship.

The King's Last Song paints a vivid portrait of Cambodia's cultural and political past and present, hewing close to history. It's absorbing, erudite and informed by meticulous research.

Ryman, a Canadian author who lives in London, is a frequent visitor to Cambodia.

A Short History of Cambodia: From Empire to Survival by John Tully (2005)

Tully sweeps across 2,000 years of ancient and modern history, serving it up in succinct, bite-size chunks from before the glory days of the Angkor "god kings" to today's flawed, strongman-led democracy. Although Cambodia once boasted a powerful empire, by the late 18th century it struggled to survive, squeezed by its Siamese (Thai) and Vietnamese neighbours. The French intervened in 1863 to see off the predators, but then colonised the country and remained for a hundred years.

The wily and autocratic King Nordom Sihanouk led the country to independence in 1953 and ran it directly or through cronies until 1970, when Cambodia "blundered into a modern dark age". That decade endured a vicious civil war, carpet bombing by the US during the Vietnam war, the Khmer Rouge nightmare – with mass murder perpetrated in pursuit of Pol Pot's "savage utopia" – and invasion and liberation by Vietnam in 1979. But Hanoi didn't pull its troops out until 1989.

Tully's very readable book tackles the complex conflicts, convoluted alliances and tumultuous events that brought the country to where it is today. Hopes of a more democratic and egalitarian society have been dashed as Cambodia is dogged by poverty, corruption and authoritarian rule – and has been largely forgotten by the world.

Tully, an Australian historian, lectures at Victoria University in Melbourne.

Read On

First They Killed My Father: A Daughter of Cambodia Remembers by Loung Ung (2000); The Rent Collector by Cameron Wright (2012); When the War Was Over: Cambodia and the Khmer Rouge Revolution by Elizabeth Becker (1986/1998); Hunters in the Dark by Lawrence Osborne (2015); Cambodia: From Pol Pot to Hun Sen and Beyond by Sebastian Strangio (2020); Dogs at the Perimeter by Madeleine Thein (2011); Sideshow: Kissinger, Nixon, and the Destruction of Cambodia by William Shawcross (1979); Never Fall Down by Patricia McCormick (2012); The Disappeared by Kim Echlin (2009)

China

The Garlic Ballads by Mo Yan (1988), translated by Howard Goldblatt

Blood, sweat and tears – and the pungent smell of garlic – run through Mo's gritty tale of penury and powerlessness in rural China. The story, set in the late-1980s, is inspired by a real incident.

Poor farmers in the ironically named Paradise County are encouraged by officials to plant garlic. But when a glut ensues, the corrupt bureaucrats, who have already lined their pockets, refuse to buy any more of the crop and it is left to rot in the fields. Facing ruin, the enraged farmers riot and burn down the county offices. Official retribution is swift and savage. The "revolt" is crushed, and the alleged ringleaders beaten and jailed. Among those held are villagers Gao Yang and Gao Ma – the latter involved in a passionate but doomed love affair – who tell their stories through flashbacks.

Mo vividly portrays the peasants' harsh existence and the greed that corrupts both families and officials – and ruins lives. That, along with his powerful, lyrical prose and tempered rage make The Garlic Ballads a fascinating and revelatory read.

Mo Yan, a pen name that means "don't speak", was a controversial winner of the 2012 Nobel prize for literature. Critics said the former People's Liberation Army officer was too close to the state. This novel, however, was banned for a time.

See also: Red Sorghum (1986); Big Breasts and Wide Hips (1996); Life and Death Are Wearing Me Out (2006), all translated by Howard Goldblatt

A Thousand Years of Good Prayers by Yiyun Li (2005)

Li's prizewinning debut collection of 10 stories delves into the lives of everyday Chinese – both at home and in the US – struggling to cope with a fast-changing China.

In Extra, Granny Lin finds herself without a job or a pension after being laid off ("honourably retired", in official parlance) from her state-owned garment factory, which has gone bust. She ends up working as a maid at a private boarding school for the children of wealthy parents. In Son, an emigrant returns from the US to find that his mother has forsaken Mao for Jesus. He, meanwhile, has to tell her that he is no longer traditional marriage material (as a sought-after Chinese-American "diamond bachelor") because he is gay. In Immortality, the most ambitious and overtly political story, a boy is born with Mao's face and is used to impersonate him in propaganda films.

Using beautifully understated prose, Li illustrates how the personal, the political and the past bear down on her protagonists' often precarious lives and make happiness elusive. These provocative and poignant portraits offer a kaleidoscope of characters who give us an inside view of China today.

Li grew up in Beijing, leaving after university to study in the US, where she now lives.

See also: The Vagrants (2009); Gold Boy, Emerald Girl (2010); Wednesday's Child (2023)

Tiger Head, Snake Tails: China Today, How It Got There and Why It Has to Change by Jonathan Fenby (2012)

This "one-stop account" of China's explosive rise tells us where the country stands at the time of writing, the route it took to get there, and where it may be heading. Behind the dazzling data – biggest, fastest-growing, most populous – Fenby lays out harsh economic and political realities.

He outlines three specific problems: corruption, which distorts the economy and skews morality; environmental degradation, which threatens ecological disaster; and a demographic time-bomb (a fast-ageing nation) with a big gender imbalance (men vastly outnumber women).

Although economic opportunities are now available, the Communist party maintains a tight rein on political freedoms. And despite hundreds of millions of people being pulled out of poverty by economic growth, stark inequalities exist as a state-linked elite has benefited most from the gains. Under the party's "authoritarian capitalism", economic expansion is essential for regime preservation, to keep a lid on dissent. Can the tiger head (the party and its vision) move relentlessly forward as the snake tails of inherent weaknesses in the system drag along the ground?

Fenby's lively first-hand reportage is augmented by sure-footed analysis, and outsiders perplexed by China will appreciate this illuminating look into the dragon's den. The author, a China-watcher for more than two decades, is a former editor of the Observer and the South China Morning Post.

See also: The Penguin History of Modern China: The Fall and Rise of a Great Power, 1850 to the Present (2008)

Read on

Wild Swans: Three Daughters of China by Jung Chang (1991); Beijing Coma by Ma Jian (2008), translated by Flora Drew; Do Not Say We Have Nothing by Madeleine Thien (2016); The Four Books by Yan Lianke (2011), translated by Carlos Rojas; China After Mao: The Rise of a Superpower by Frank Dikötter (2022); Eat the Buddha: Life and Death in a Tibetan Town by Barbara Demick (2020); Red Memory: The Afterlives of China's Cultural Revolution by Tania Branigan (2023); Private Revolutions: Coming of Age in a New China by Yuan Yang (2024)

India

Midnight's Children by Salman Rushdie (1981)

Saleem Sinai, the novel's narrator, is born at the stroke of midnight on 15 August 1947 – the exact moment of India's independence from Britain. He finds himself "handcuffed to history, my destinies indissolubly chained to those of my country". All the 1,001 babies born in that midnight hour have a mystical bond and are endowed with magical powers. Saleem's is being able to enter the minds of others and see events through their eyes, be they famous historical figures such as Mahatma Gandhi and Jawaharlal Nehru, a humble beggar, or his own parents.

Rushdie's exuberant and witty magic-realist masterpiece reveals a soaring imagination, melding the personal with the historical and fact with fantasy as it tells the coming-of-age stories of both child and country. Saleem is a personable guide through key events in post-independence India: the bloody turmoil of partition; Bangladesh's painful secession from Pakistan with New Delhi's help; Indira Gandhi's "emergency rule" of the 1970s, when she flirted with dictatorship.

This landmark novel put Indian fiction written in English firmly on the literary map. It won the Booker prize in 1981 and was voted the Booker of Bookers in 1993 and in 2008, on the award's 25th and 40th anniversaries respectively. The Indian-born author, who lived in the UK for years, now lives in New York.

See also: Shame (1983); Shalimar the Clown (2005); The Moor's Last Sigh (1995)

A Fine Balance by Rohinton Mistry (1995)

Mistry's novel is set in 1970s Bombay, during the repressive "emergency" period. It focuses on four main characters who are struggling to survive, and whose lives become inextricably linked. They are an uncle and nephew, "untouchables" who have fled caste violence in their village and reinvented themselves as tailors; an impoverished middle-class Parsi widow striving to preserve her independence; and a student renting a room in the widow's tiny flat who is forced to learn new skills as his family's business is failing.

The widow, Dina Dalal, employs the tailors to make clothes for an export company in an effort to boost her fragile finances, and the four protagonists form something of a family bond. The novel – laced with black humour – follows their precarious existence as they learn to "maintain a fine balance between hope and despair" and show great resilience in the face of mounting chaos and calamity.

Mistry vividly portrays Indian life and offers an unflinching look at some of its harsh realities: forced sterilisation, caste prejudice, corruption, slum clearances and grinding poverty. Although epic in its ambition, the novel's lyricism and understated passion convey intimacy. The author creates rich, credible characters to tell a bewitching and heartbreaking story.

Mistry, born and raised in Bombay (Mumbai), has lived in Canada since 1975.

See also: Such a Long Journey (1991); Tales from Firozsha Baag (1987)

In Spite of the Gods: The Strange Rise of Modern India by Edward Luce (2006)

"In India, things are never as good or as bad as they seem," a fellow journalist tells Luce. It's a healthy scepticism the author takes on board in his perceptive and witty, warts-and-all view of modern India. Luce explores the "schizophrenic" economy, where past practices clash with future ambitions; the ubiquitous bureaucracy that profits from endemic corruption; caste struggles that foster voting allegiances; intolerant Hindu nationalism and its attempts to rewrite history; dynastic – and sycophantic – politics; the Muslim minority and the Kashmir "problem"; and the foreign policy "triangular dance" with the US and China.

At the heart of the country's forward march Luce finds an ongoing struggle between tradition and modernity. And as India jockeys for a place at the world's top table – with its fast-growing economy, nuclear capability, massive population and hi-tech skills – he notes that "almost 300 million Indians can never be sure where their next meal will come from". Luce succeeds admirably in his aim of providing "an unsentimental evaluation of contemporary India". And although he is far from uncritical, his affection for the country shines through.

The author, a Financial Times journalist, was the newspaper's Delhi-based, south Asia bureau chief between 2001 and 2005.

Read on

India After Gandhi: A History by Ramchandra Guha (2007/2023); A Suitable Boy by Vikram Seth (1993); The Many Lives of Syeda X: The Story of an Unknown Indian by Neha Dixit (2024); The White Tiger by Aravind Adiga (2008); The God of Small Things by Arundhati Roy (1997); The Fertile Earth by Ruthvika Rao (2024); Quarterlife by Devika Rege (2023); The Lowland by Jhumpa Lahiri (2013); A Burning by Meghan Majumdar (2020); Train to Pakistan by Khushwant Singh (1956); India: A History by John Keay (2000/2010); Behind the Beautiful Forevers: Life, Death and Hope in a Mumbai Slum by Katherine Boo (2012)

Indonesia

This Earth of Mankind by Pramoedya Ananta Toer (1980), translated by Max Lane

The first book in Pramoedya's epic Buru quartet, set in the waning years of Dutch colonial rule, is a bittersweet coming-of-age novel. The narrator and central character, Minke, is a gifted 18-year-old Javanese from an aristocratic family who goes to a prestigious Dutch school where he is the only "native" Indonesian. His talent and self-confidence arouse the envy and contempt of his "pure" (European) and "Indo" (Indo-European) classmates.

Pramoedya quietly excoriates colonial society, in which Indonesians suffer indignities and injustices because social standing and rights depend on the amount of European blood in one's veins. With his refusal to accept his place in a racially stratified society, Minke embodies incipient Indonesian nationalism. He falls in love with the beautiful daughter of an absent Dutch father and an astute, strong-willed native "concubine". But their hopes for the future run up against Javanese prejudices and hardline Dutch colonial law.

Pramoedya was imprisoned by the Dutch and then by the Indonesian government under Suharto. He spent 14 years in a penal colony on Buru Island, composing and memorising This Earth by repeating it to fellow prisoners after he was denied writing materials. The book was banned by the regime shortly after publication in 1980, but is freely available today. The author died in 2006.

See also: The Buru Quartet: This Earth of Mankind, Child of All Nations, Footsteps, House of Glass (1980-88), translated by Max Lane; The Mute's Soliloquy: A Memoir (1999), translated by Willem Samuels

Beauty Is a Wound by Eka Kurniawan (2002), translated by Annie Tucker

"One afternoon on a weekend in March, Dewi Ayu rose from her grave after being dead for twenty-one years." The Marquesian opening sentence launches Eka's debut novel – a sprawling, bawdy and violent tale recounting the family saga of Dewi Ayu, a stunningly beautiful mixed-race prostitute, and her four daughters in the fictional town of Halimunda.

The exuberant, multi-generational story bounds across much of Indonesia's turbulent 20th century. A rich tapestry of magic realism, folklore and personal drama weaves in key historical events, from rapacious Dutch colonialism to cruel Japanese occupation, painful birth at independence, a blood-soaked coup and massacres in 1965, and Suharto's repressive rule.

The extraordinary beauty of Dewi Ayu and her family (all except for her fourth daughter, called Beauty, who is singularly unattractive) is often less a blessing and more a curse as their lives are buffeted by political and personal upheaval. According to her: "There is no curse more terrible than to give birth to a pretty female in a world of men as nasty as dogs in heat."

Eka doesn't stint on the sex and violence – or the dark humour. The time-bending structure and extensive cast of characters can occasionally be challenging, but this audacious novel zings with passion and readers who persist with its rich, complex tale will be rewarded.

A celebrated Indonesian novelist and screenwriter, Eka is seen as a literary successor to Pramaoedya.
See also: Man Tiger (2004), translated by Labodalih Sembiring

In the Time of Madness: Indonesia on the Edge of Chaos by Richard Lloyd Parry (1980)

"This book is about violence, and about being afraid," says Parry, as his riveting, eye-witness account presents a slice of Indonesian history during a turbulent and chaotic time. Near the end of the 20th century, Indonesia was emerging from three decades of Suharto's dictatorship, and pent-up frustrations were being released. "A struggle [is] taking place between something old, murderous and corrupt, and something new," the author writes.

The book is divided into three sections, chronicling events to which Parry is witness: savage ethnic conflict in Borneo; massive student protests in the capital, Jakarta, that bring down Suharto; and bloody violence in East Timor around the referendum on its independence from Indonesia.

This deeply personal, sometimes harrowing account of Indonesia's implosion lacks a central focus, but more than makes up for it in gripping narrative. Parry proves to be a lucid and intelligent guide to navigating the complexities of this vast archipelago with its various languages, ethnicities and religions. And his pungent reportage is of a kind that remains long after the headlines have faded.

British journalist Parry is Asia editor of the Times based in Tokyo, but he has often visited Indonesia to report for the Independent and the Times newspapers.

Read on

The Year of Living Dangerously by Christopher J Koch (1978); Indonesia, Etc: Exploring the Improbable Nation by Elizabeth Pisani (2014); Revolusi: Indonesia and the Birth of the Modern World by David Van Reybrouck (2020), translated by David Colmer and David McKay; Map of the Invisible World by Tash Aw (2009); Home by

Leila S Chudori (2012), translated by John H McGlynn; The Rainbow Troops by Andrea Hirata (2005), translated by Angie Kilbane; Saman by Ayu Utami (1998), translated by Pamela Allen; Durga/Umayi by YB Mangunwijaya (1991), translated by Ward Keeler

Malaysia

The Garden of Evening Mists by Tan Twan Eng (2012)

In the 1980s, recently retired supreme court judge Yun Ling Teoh returns to the eponymous garden in Malaysia's Cameron Highlands where she spent time more than 30 years earlier. Diagnosed with a neurological disorder, she is losing her memory and needs to reckon with her past.

As a teenager, Yun Ling, along with her sister, spent the second world war in a Japanese slave labour camp, of which she was the only survivor. After the war she visited the highlands with the intention of creating a memorial garden for her beloved sister, and met the mysterious Aritomo Nakamura, once the emperor of Japan's gardener. Despite her hatred of the Japanese, she became his apprentice – and then his lover.

As Yun Ling recalls her past, the story shifts back and forth between different time periods: the late 1980s; the 1950s during the communist insurgency in British Malaya; and the second world war under Japanese occupation. It's a tale of love, loss, memory and forgetting, told with a quiet, lyrical intensity.

This novel, Tan's second – emotionally absorbing, atmospheric and tinged with an effortless melancholy – confirms him as a leading Malaysian literary light. It was shortlisted for the 2012 Man Booker prize and won the Man Asian literary prize that same year.

The Penang-born former lawyer divides his time between Malaysia and South Africa.

See also: The Gift of Rain (2007); House of Doors (2023); The South (2025)

The Harmony Silk Factory by Tash Aw (2005)

Aw's alluring debut novel is set mainly in 1940s Malaya, under British colonial rule, as the Japanese prepare to invade. The central character is the enigmatic Johnny Lim, a Chinese-Malay textile merchant and owner of the Harmony Silk Factory. Is he an upstanding businessman and war hero who protected his community during the Japanese occupation or a collaborator, black marketeer and killer, who betrayed his communist comrades?

The story is told in three overlapping narratives that have distinct voices and different interpretations of the past. The first section is by Johnny's estranged son Jasper, who is convinced his father was a trickster and a traitor. The second, by Johnny's wife, the beautiful Snow Soong, is in the form of a diary written in 1941 during the couple's strange, belated honeymoon to the

Seven Maidens Islands accompanied by a mysterious Japanese professor and two Englishmen. One of the English expats is Peter Wormwood, Johnny's best friend, who is the final storyteller, looking back many years after the war as he lives out his days in a care home.

Aw's intense, intricate novel has prose sometimes as lush as Malaya's tropical landscape, which keeps the pages turning. However, he doesn't tie up all the loose ends, leaving the reader with work to do.

The Malaysian author lives in Britain in what he calls "voluntary exile".

See also: We, the Survivors (2019); Map of the Invisible World (2009)

Crossroads: A Popular History of Malaysia and Singapore by Jim Baker (1999/2020)

This comprehensive history book's running to an updated fourth edition testifies to its enduring relevance and popularity. It's an accessible and lively account – social, economic and political – of the Malay peninsula from its earliest inhabitants to the present day. The peninsula's location at the crossroads of trade routes brought the attention of foreign powers. Early on China and India had an impact, and later the European colonial powers, with the British eventually gaining control in the early 19th century.

Japan's defeat of the British in Malaya and people's suffering under its occupation during the war "were death knells for colonialism", leading to independence in 1957 – in the wake of a communist insurgency. Malaya (later Malaysia) emerged as "a multicultural society with significant racial divisions" between Malays, Chinese and Indians, and even today ethnic identity is "at the core of most public discourse".

Baker examines key events in post-independence Malaysia along with the more recent challenges of Islamisation and globalisation. He closes with the 2018 election, which saw the long-retired Mahathir Mohamad return as prime minister fronting the opposition to his former party. A result, Baker says, that "turned politics on its head". A rich source of information, Crossroads is a primer *sine pari* on Malaysia and Singapore.

Baker, an American who has spent most of his life in Singapore, teaches at the American school there.

Read on

Evening Is the Whole Day by Preeta Samarasan (2008); The Weight of Our Sky by Hanna Alkaf (2019); The Rice Mother by Rani Manicka (2002); And the Rain My Drink by Han Suyin (1956); The Storm We Made by Vanessa Chan (2024); The Night Tiger by Yangsze Choo (2019); Lake Like a Mirror by Ho Sok Fong (2014), translated by Natascha Bruce

Myanmar (Burma)

The Glass Palace by Amitav Ghosh (2000)

From the British invasion of Mandalay in 1885, this lively novel of love, loss and longing sweeps across more than 100 years of history in Burma, India and Malaya. Rajkumar Raha, an 11-year-old penniless orphan, is witness to the British attack on Burma's royal capital. As he mingles with looters in the palace, he spies – and is instantly smitten by – 10-year-old Dolly, a maid, who accompanies the Burmese monarchs as they are sent into exile in India. Years later, having become rich through the teak trade, Raha goes in search of Dolly.

The fast-moving story links three families through three generations as they are buffeted by the region's political turmoil and social upheaval. It's storytelling on a grand scale – through empire, two world wars, independence struggles and Myanmar's military regime – threaded with a cast of characters who are both compelling and credible.

The Glass Palace serves up more than a sumptuous family saga. By giving voice to the Burmese and Indians who are witness to the waxing and waning of empire, Ghosh offers an intelligent, thought-provoking and ultimately damning portrait of British colonialism and imperialism. This meticulously researched and luminous novel took five years to write, with the seed of the story planted by tales of the Indian author's own family's history.

See also: The Ibis Trilogy – Sea of Poppies (2008), River of Smoke (2011), Flood of Fire (2012); The Hungry Tide (2004)

The Lizard Cage by Karen Connelly (2005)

Connelly's gritty novel about a political prisoner is a paean to the human spirit and a savage indictment of Burma's military regime. Teza, a student activist and popular protest singer, is in solitary confinement in a prison complex known as The Cage. Arrested during the pro-democracy protests in 1988, which were brutally suppressed, he has served seven years of a 20-year term. Under the harsh prison regime, Teza suffers constant hunger – using lizards to supplement his diet – and vicious beatings. He falls back on his Buddhist faith and fond memories of bygone days to endure the hardship.

Senior jailer Chit Naing, troubled by his conscience, is sympathetic to Teza's plight, but junior jailer "Handsome" is sadistic and violent. Also in The Cage is Little Brother, an orphaned boy raised in the prison, who survives by killing rats and selling them to the hungry prisoners. He becomes Teza's server, delivering his prison meals. When the chief warden tries to frame Teza in a bid to increase his sentence, the novel turns thriller as both prisoner and boy face grave danger. Connelly pulls no punches on the horrors of prison life, but offers the tentative bond formed between Teza and Little Brother as some small hope in this powerful tale.

The author, a Canadian poet and writer, lived for two years among Burmese exiles on the Thailand-Myanmar border. *See also: Burmese Lessons – A True Love Story (2010)*

The River of Lost Footsteps: A Personal History of Burma by Thant Myint-U (2006)

Thant weaves some of his family history into this comprehensive chronicle of Burma's past. It harks back to the country's foundations, but comes into its own with the British assault and occupation of the country in 1885 – a watershed year that ushered in the modern age. The monarchy was abolished, old certainties disappeared, and society was "aggressively transformed". Wounded national pride was dealt a further blow when Britain ruled the country as an appendage of India.

Burma emerged at independence in 1948 devastated by the second world war, with some of its top leaders recently assassinated, and heralding the outbreak of the world's longest-running civil war – hardly a promising start. Thant relates how the fledgling democracy was dogged by turbulent politics, foreign incursions and local insurgencies.

General Ne Win's coup in 1962 brought the shutters down on the outside world, and Burma descended into decades of paranoid military dictatorship. Despite huge protests in 1988 and the emergence of the generals' nemesis, Aung San Suu Kyi, the military remains largely in control, only relinquishing some powers after elections in the 2010s.

"We fail to consider history at our peril," says Thant in this subtle and engaging portrait of the country, which should be mandatory reading for anyone wanting to understand modern-day Myanmar.

Thant, born in the US to Burmese parents, is the grandson of the former UN secretary general U Thant.

See also: The Hidden History of Burma (2019)

Read on

On the Shadow Tracks: A Journey through Occupied Myanmar by Clare Hammond (2024); Burmese Days by George Orwell (1934); A Savage Dreamland: Journeys in Burma by David Eimer (2019); Miss Burma by Charmaine Craig (2017); Blood, Dreams and Gold: The Changing Face of Burma by Richard Cockett (2015); The Lady And The Peacock: The Life of Aung San Suu Kyi of Burma by Peter Popham (2011); From the Land of Green Ghosts by Pascal Khoo Thwe (2002); The Invisible Ones by Karel van Loon (2006), translated by David Colmer; The Road to Wanting by Wendy Law-Yone (2010); Smile As They Bow by Nu Nu Yi (1994), translated by Thi Thi Aye and Alfred Birnbaum

North Korea

The Accusation: Forbidden Stories From Inside North Korea by Bandi (2014), translated by Deborah Smith

Seven short stories, each pointing an accusing finger at the ruling regime, shine a light on North Korea's "truly fathomless darkness". Written between 1989 and 1995, in the final years of Kim Il-sung's rule, these are tragic tales of everyday people whose lives are brutalised by a cruel and capricious regime: a man is denied a travel permit to visit his dying mother; a wife survives on "dog food" as she struggles to feed her husband during a famine; a son confronts his father, a party loyalist, about the government's fake truths and propaganda theatre; a family whose child is terrified by the huge, ubiquitous posters of Marx and Kim is banished from the city for being anti-revolutionary.

In this dystopian world, the political "sins" of fathers – perceived dissidence or failings – are visited on entire families. They pay dearly, and are tainted for generations. In the midst of dashed hopes and broken dreams, the flame of hope barely flickers. These are indeed, as the book's subtitle says, forbidden stories.

Bandi, meaning "firefly" in Korean, is the pseudonym of a prominent North Korean writer still living in his country. The manuscript was smuggled across the border to South Korea sandwiched between official propaganda books, among them The Collected Works of Kim Il-sung.

The Orphan Master's Son by Adam Johnson (2012)

Johnson's epic, disquieting novel follows the fortunes of every-man Jun Do (John Doe), from humble beginnings – raised in an orphanage run by his single father – to impersonating a famous military hero and becoming a love rival of North Korea's leader, Kim Jong-il.

The book's first half is an intimate biography of Jun Do. Forced by famine into the military, he is trained to fight in the dark in the tunnels under the demilitarised border zone. He graduates from soldier to kidnapper for the state, to spy. But, following an unsuccessful mission to Texas, he falls foul of the regime and is sent to a prison camp. In the second half, Jun Do embarks on a wild, surreal journey. He escapes from prison, assuming a new identity that takes him into the upper echelons of society and sees him vying with the Dear Leader for the affections of the nation's favourite actress, Sun Moon.

Part political thriller, part parody, part love story, this genre-breaking novel opens a window on the secretive state where people live in constant fear, and deploys dark humour to portray the absurd realities and grim horrors of life. A fascination with propaganda, and its use in a totalitarian state, drew the American author to researching and visiting North Korea. This, Johnson's second novel, won the Pulitzer prize for fiction in 2013.

See also: Fortune Smiles (2015)

Nothing to Envy: Real Lives in North Korea by Barbara Demick (2009)

The title comes from a propaganda song, We Have Nothing to Envy in This World, but Demick's riveting and rigorously researched book tells a very different story. It follows the lives of six North Koreans who eventually "defected" to the south, and weaves in historical context.

Although heartbreaking and harrowing in equal measure, it humanises the country's citizens, of whom so little is known. Through them we get the inside story on the absolute obedience enforced by the state; the rigid caste system based on perceived loyalty to the regime; the terror of being denounced by neighbours for trivial "offences"; the gulag-like labour camps; and the cult of Kim, which deifies the leader.

A famine in the 1990s and economic collapse proved to be a turning point. The state abandoned its citizens, who were forced to eat grass and tree bark to survive, and between 600,000 and 2 million people died. Loyalties wavered, and hunger gave people new motivation to escape. However, Demick sees little prospect of regime change. Hopes were raised when the young, western-schooled Kim Jong-un was picked to be the next of Kim. But, like his father Kim Jong-il, he prioritised weapons over food.

This is impressive reportage, and an eye-opener on a closed world. US journalist Demick was the Los Angeles Times bureau chief in South Korea for six years, and reported extensively on North Korea. *See also: Eat the Buddha: Life and Death in a Tibetan Town (2020)*

Read on

Friend: A Novel from North Korea by Paek Nam-nyong (2020), translated by Immanuel Kim; Beasts of a Little Land by Juhea Kim (2021); The Impossible State: North Korea, Past and Future by Victor Cha (2012/2023); The Great Successor: The Secret Rise and Rule of Kim Jong Un by Anna Fifield (2019); The Girl With Seven Names by Hyeonseo Lee with David John (2015); How I Became a North Korean by Krys Lee (2016); The Sorcerer of Pyongyang by Marcel Theroux (2022); Accidental Tyrant: The Life of Kim Il-sung by Fyodor Tertitskiy (2025)

Pakistan

A Case of Exploding Mangoes by Mohammed Hanif (2008)

Hanif's darkly comic debut novel swirls around a real event, the 1988 crash of a plane carrying Pakistan's strongman president, General Zia ul-Haq, top military brass and the US ambassador. All those on board died. Who was responsible for the incident remains a mystery, though conspiracy theories abound. This exuberant political satire (and whodunit), thick with plots and subplots, takes aim at the bumbling and brutal military rulers as well as Zia's Islamic fundamentalism and backing (with US slush funds) of anti-Russian jihadis in neighbouring Afghanistan.

Ten years into his repressive regime, Zia is an increasingly paranoid and insecure figure. He's not just preoccupied with his safety, but also with his acceptance speech for the Nobel peace prize that he fantasises being awarded for combating communism. His enemies, meanwhile, are conspiring against him. The novel's main narrator, junior airforce officer Ali Shigri, blames the dictator for his father's death and is bent on revenge. Others too, among them ambitious generals and trade unionists, have plans to rid the country of its turbulent president.

Fizzing with wit and energy – and replete with rich, colourful characters – Hanif's clever chronicle of a death foretold is an immensely enjoyable read.

Hanif trained as a fighter pilot in Pakistan before deciding to become a journalist. During a 12-year spell in Britain he worked for the BBC, returning to Pakistan in 2008.

See also: Our Lady of Alice Bhatti (2011)

In Other Rooms, Other Wonders by Daniyal Mueenuddin (2009)

The intricacies and inequities of Pakistan's class system are exposed in Mueenuddin's elegantly crafted collection of short stories. The eight loosely linked tales, set around the wealthy, landowning Harouni family in Punjab province, invade living rooms, bedrooms, kitchens and servants quarters to illuminate a changing world where modernity is knocking at the gates of feudalism.

The lives portrayed of servants, scions, peasants and lovers all have the ring of authenticity. In a landscape darkened by corruption and injustice, those caught at the wrong end survive as best they can. Women battle patriarchy and misogyny, sometimes trading sex for security – but the benefits can be transitory and the consequences tragic.

In Nawabdin Electrician, a handyman flourishes as a result of his "technique for cheating the electric company by slowing down the revolutions of electric meters"; in Provide, Provide, the corrupt manager of an estate boasts that "I have so much because I took what I wanted"; in the eponymous title story a poor, young woman becomes the ageing Harouni's mistress, but is banished by his daughters on the patriarch's death. This delicately detailed insight into modern-day Pakistan will have readers lingering in these rooms long after the last page has been turned.

Mueenuddin trained and worked as a lawyer in the US before returning to his native Pakistan to look after the family farm.

Pakistan: A Hard Country by Anatol Lieven (2011)

It's said that Pakistan's politics are steered by the three As: the army, Allah and America. Lieven's meticulously researched and impressively well-sourced book examines these three and more: corruption, venal politicians, economic backwardness, ethnic and regional divisions, the oppression of women, inequality.

Although well aware of the many challenges facing the country, he eschews the cliches of Pakistan being "on the brink" or a "failed state". The entrenched "feudal" system of kinship and patronage, Lieven argues, contributes to the state's stability and resilience – but it also stymies attempts by governments, both democratic and dictatorial, to institute reforms essential to the nation's long-term survival. He judges the army as being Pakistan's most efficient institution, though he decries its obsession with old foe, and fellow nuclear club member, India and its support for jihadi groups.

The gravest threats to the country are cited as being the US presence in Afghanistan, fuelling anti-Americanism and Islamist insurgency, and environmental disaster unleashed by climate change.

In his attempt to show how Pakistan works, Lieven passes with panache, capturing the country "in all its complex patchwork of light and shadow". Conscientious and fair-minded, his affection for and knowledge of this much misunderstood nation are palpable.

The British former journalist, who has reported from south Asia, teaches international relations at King's College London.

Read on

The Nine Lives of Pakistan: Dispatches from a Divided Nation by Declan Walsh (2020); The Reluctant Fundamentalist by Mohsin Hamid (2007); Kartography by Kamila Shamsie (2001); The Golden

Legend by Nadeem Aslam (2017); Cracking India (formerly Ice Candy Man) by Bapsi Sidhwa (1988); Shame by Salman Rushdie (1983); Karachi Vice by Samira Shackle (2021)

Philippines

Dusk by F Sionil José (1984)

Dusk is the first novel in José's acclaimed Rosales Saga, five books that follow the fortunes of one family through 100 years of Philippine history. Dusk begins during the last days of Spanish rule at the end of the 19th century and ends with the entry of the United States as the new colonial master. It relates the trials and tribulations of the Samson family as Spanish rough justice drives them off their land and forces them to flee their village. On their long, arduous journey to find new land to farm, the extended family are harried by other ethnic groups, bandits and the colonial Guardia Civil. They finally settle in what becomes Rosales.

The main character, Eustaquio (Istak) Samson, although a farmer's son, is taken under the wing of a liberal Spanish priest and learns Spanish and Latin. But eventually he is impelled to join the struggle for independence, which transforms him from poor farmer and would-be seminarian into rebel fighter

José's engaging and sympathetic storytelling puts the reader right alongside the protagonists as they struggle for a better life. The novel vividly captures the oppression and simmering discontent of Filipinos under colonial rule, showing how the unifying struggle against imperialism forges Philippine identity.

José is one of the most widely read Filipino authors, and the Rosales novels, set in his home town, are bestsellers in his native land.

See also: Ermita: A Filipino Novel (1988)

Ilustrado by Miguel Syjuco (2010)

Syjuco's sparkling and strikingly ambitious debut novel begins with the suspicious drowning in New York's Hudson river of a self-exiled Philippine literary legend, Crispin Salvador. Was it suicide or murder? A controversial figure at home, Salvador attracted as many foes as he did fans. The manuscript of his final work – an exposé of corruption among the Filipino ruling elite, which is also an attempt to settle scores with his critics – has vanished.

A Salvador acolyte – named Miguel Syjuco, like the author – decides to find out what really happened to his literary mentor and to track down the missing manuscript. The mission takes Miguel back to his home town, Manila, which is also home to Salvador's biggest successes and setbacks.

This evocative tale of modern Manila, spiced with philosophical musings and wry humour, leaps around Philippine culture, history and politics. The story is told through a multi-layered and dizzying array of sources, among them blogs, newspaper cuttings, emails, extracts from Salvador's books, Miguel's own writings, and jokes. The novel's sprawling structure and style is sometimes overwhelming, but despite the bumps in the road it's worth the ride.

Syjuco, born and raised in the Philippines, now lives in Canada. Ilustrado won the Man Asian literary prize in 2008 while it was still an unpublished manuscript.

See also: I Was the President's Mistress!! (2022)

America's Boy: The Marcoses and the Philippines by James Hamilton-Paterson (1998)

After its long stretch under two foreign powers, Spain and the US – 300 years in a Spanish convent and 50 years of Hollywood, as the adage goes – ended in 1946, post-independence Philippines emerged as a flawed democracy. Hamilton-Paterson contends it's a system run by oligarchs and defined by corruption and cronyism; "goons, guns and gold" all play their part. The US, meanwhile, continued to wield enormous clout.

In this biography of the Marcos dictatorship, although no apologist for Ferdinand and Imelda, the author controversially claims the regime was not an aberration, but represented Filipino political practices that preceded it and continue to this day. Ferdinand Marcos, "America's boy", had practically unconditional US backing. Washington, seeing him as a bulwark against the "communist threat", turned a blind eye to his kleptomania and authoritarianism. Growing local opposition and a thaw in the cold war finally induced the US to withdraw support in 1986, leading to Marcos's ousting. But, says Hamilton-Paterson, with the "saintly" Cory Aquino replacing Marcos after the "people's revolution", only the players changed, not the system.

Hamilton-Paterson elicits information from Marcos's friends, foes and family (including his wife Imelda), and his blending of personalities and politics delivers an insightful, entertaining history. The British writer, having lived on and off in the Philippines for three decades, brings an insider's knowledge to the story. *See also: Playing With Water: Alone on a Philippine Island (1987)*

Read on

Smaller and Smaller Circles by FH Batacan (2015); Some People Need Killing: A Memoir of Murder in the Philippines by Patricia Evangelista (2023); Noli Me Tángere (Touch Me Not) by José Rizal (1887), translated by Harold Augenbraum; Insurrecto by Gina Apostol (2018); State of War by Ninotchka Rosca (1988); America Is Not the Heart by Elaine Castillo (2018); How to Stand Up to a Dictator by Maria Ressa (2023); The Making of the Modern Philippines: Pieces of a Jigsaw State by Philip Bowring (2022); In the Country by Mia Alvar (2015); Dogeaters by Jessica Hagedorn (1990)

South Korea

Human Acts by Han Kang (2014), translated by Deborah Smith

Han's novel examines the 1980 Gwangju uprising and its aftermath. That year, the military government crushed student-led pro-democracy protests in the city, with the army beating, torturing and killing hundreds of civilians.

The story focuses on Dong-ho, a 15-year-old schoolboy who goes looking for his best friend's corpse and gets caught up in the violence. The tale is threaded together through the different perspectives of people affected by the bloody events: Dong-ho, his mother, the spirit of his dead friend, a female factory worker, an editor facing censorship, a prisoner who is tortured, and finally a writer, who is the author herself. The human acts revealed encompass courage, altruism and sacrifice, as well as unbelievable cruelty and evil.

In equal measure haunting and harrowing – Han unflinchingly describes the army's brutality and torture – the novel looks at how the atrocity still reverberates in South Korea. With its beautifully composed, understated prose, this stunning book is a fitting tribute to those who lost their lives in the pursuit of freedom, and deserves to be widely read.

Gwangju-born Han's parents moved to Seoul in 1980, when she was nine years old, just months before the uprising. So her tale is both personal and political. Her novel The Vegetarian won the Man Booker International prize in 2016. And in 2024 Han was awarded the Nobel prize for literature "for her intense poetic prose that confronts historical traumas and exposes the fragility of human life".

*See also: The Vegetarian (2007), translated by Deborah Smith;
We Do Not Part (2025), translated by E Yaewon and Paige
Aniyah Morris*

White Chrysanthemum by Mary Lynn Bracht (2018)

In 1943, during Japan's occupation of Korea, 16-year-old Hana
– a *haenyeo*, a female sea diver – distracts Japanese soldiers on
the beach to save her younger sister Emi, who is hiding. Hana is
abducted and forced into sexual slavery as a "comfort woman"
for Japanese troops during the war – a fate shared by tens of
thousands of Korean women and girls.

Fast forward to 2011, and Emi, still haunted by her sister's
sacrifice, has never given up trying to find Hana. She has travelled
to Seoul to join the women protesting in front of the Japanese
embassy seeking justice for past atrocities. The novel flits back
and forth between 1943 and 2011, telling the stories of the two
sisters in alternate chapters. Hana is mercilessly abused and
incarcerated in a Manchuria brothel. Being a *haenyeo*, who are
known for their resilience, she never gives up hope of escaping
and making her way back to her family. Emi, meanwhile, is for
ever burdened by the anguish of losing her sister.

A bristling fury at the injustices perpetrated by the Japanese
propels the story as Bracht shines a light on a dark chapter in
Korean history. Her captivating debut novel will pull at you
heartstrings; it will also fill you with rage. The title is apt: the

white chrysanthemum is a symbol of mourning in Korea. The author, a Korean-American, lives in London.

Korea: The Impossible Country by Daniel Tudor (2012/2018)

Within a generation after the Korean war South Korea went from being a poor, devastated country into an economic power and vibrant democracy. But before it got there it had endured oppressive Japanese colonial rule, which ended after 35 years with Tokyo's defeat in the second world war; the division of the Korean peninsula into North Korea and South Korea; invasion by the North and civil war; and decades of military dictatorship.

Tudor contends that "the most impressive story of nation-building of the last century" has been unfairly overlooked because the west tends to focus on South Korea's neighbours: the North Korean problem, China's growth and Japan's cultural power. He aims to set things right.

To explain the country's "amazing rise from the ashes", the author delves into its history, culture and politics. He highlights two impressive achievements: the economic "miracle" in which GDP per capita soared from $100 in 1960 to $33,000 today, and the political miracle of finally dispensing with dictatorship, following elections in 1987. Success has come at a cost, though. The pressure to achieve high standards of education, pursue successful careers and conform to societal "norms" has engendered intense competitiveness, high levels of stress and the world's second-highest suicide rate.

Tudor's accessible and engaging book certainly delivers on his stated intention of offering a "way into Korea for the curious". The British journalist has lived in Seoul for more than a decade and was the Economist's Korea correspondent.

Read on

Beasts of a Little Land by Juhea Kim (2021); Kim Jiyoung, Born 1982 by Cho Nam-joo (2016), translated by Jamie Chang; Mater 2-10 by Hwang Sok-yong (2020), translated by Sora Kim-Russell and Yongjae Josephine Bae; Pachinko by Min Jin Lee (2017); Please Look After Mother by Kyung-sook Shin (2008), translated by Chi-young Kim; Shoko's Smile by Choi Eunyoung (2016), translated by Sung Ryu; Shrimp to Whale: South Korea – From the Forgotten War to K-Pop by Ramon Pacheco Pardo (2022); If I Had Your Face by Frances Cha (2020); Your Republic is Calling You by Young-ha Kim (2006), translated by Chi-young Kim

Sri Lanka

The Seven Moons of Maali Almeida by Shehan Karunatilaka (2022)

Karunatilaka's exuberant, genre-busting novel won the Booker prize in 2022. Set in the 1980s, amid the country's ferocious civil war, it's a scathing state-of-Sri-Lanka satire as well as a whodunnit, magic realist fable, ghost story and tale of gay love – all sprinkled with dark humour.

Maali Almeida, the son of a Sinhalese father and Eurasian burgher-Tamil mother, is a cynical war photographer, habitual gambler and promiscuous gay man. A witness to the savagery of the conflict, he has taken pictures "that will bring down governments. Photos that could stop wars." At the start of the novel, he wakes up dead, finding himself in a sort of afterlife purgatory (the In Between), crowded with ghosts and ghouls, many of whom were victims of the war. If he can't uncover his killer within seven nights (seven moons), his soul will be be stuck in purgatory for ever, at the mercy of the demons clamouring for it.

It's no easy task, as murder suspects abound: the country is plagued by death squads, suicide bombers, the Sri Lankan army and criminal thugs. To find the answer, Maali must direct his friends to the hidden cache of photos at his home in Colombo, which reveal atrocities committed by the government and others.

The novel's second-person narrative creates a sense of immediacy and intimacy, and drives this ambitious and absorbing story along at a brisk pace. Karunatilaka is a Sri Lankan writer and occasional rock band bass player.
See also: Chinaman (2010)

Brotherless Night by VV Ganeshananthan (2023)
This searing coming-of-age story takes place mainly in the northern city of Jaffna during the early years of the civil war. Told from the

perspective of a young Tamil woman, Sashikala "Sashi" Kulenthiren, an aspiring doctor, it's both haunting and heartbreaking, and brings the conflict up close and personal.

The bloody repression unleashed by the Sri Lankan government against the Tamil community precipitates the birth of armed militant groups clamouring for secession, foremost among them the ruthless Tamil Tigers. Sashi grapples with the escalating violence, which eventually tears apart her family – and her country. The young medical student, her four beloved brothers and her parents are caught in the crossfire of the conflict, and must deal with the moral ambiguities that arise as the line between right and wrong is blurred. "It does not matter if you cannot imagine the future," Sashi posits. "Still relentless, it comes."

After one brother is killed in anti-Tamil riots and two others, along with their best friend, join the Tigers, Sashi finds her life disrupted as she struggles to navigate her way through political turmoil and conflicting loyalties.

Epic in its aspiration yet intimate in its telling, the beautiful writing and the narrative's close adherence to actual events – drawing on 16 years of research – make this novel a triumph of historical fiction. It comes trailing accolades and awards.

Ganeshananthan, a Sri Lankan-American, teaches at the University of Minnesota.

See also: Love Marriage (2008)

This Divided Island: Stories from the Sri Lankan War by Samanth Subramanian (2014)

The Sri Lankan army's victory over the Tamil Tigers in 2009 ended a 26-year civil war. But what had almost three decades of bitter, bloody conflict done to the country's soul? In the wake of the war, Subramanian travels across the island to find out. In his rich tapestry of reportage and travelogue he hears from belligerents, their backers and those caught in the crossfire.

Britain's colonial policy sowed the seeds of ethnic strife by favouring the minority Tamils. Following independence in 1948, the majority Sinhalese responded with laws that discriminated against Tamils. The increasingly muscular nationalism also triggered anti-Tamil pogroms and led to the founding of the Tamil Tigers, who sought a breakaway state. The war – under cold-blooded leaders – saw atrocities committed by both sides, and in the final crushing of the Tigers more than 40,000 civilians died as the army closed in. The cliched description of the island is of "a teardrop in the Indian Ocean", But Subramanian sees it as also resembling a hand grenade.

Fear and anger still ripple through the island; there has been no reckoning or reconciliation; and the truth continues to be heavily contested territory. This balanced account of the war and its aftermath explores the trauma that visited the island and the shadow it casts over people's lives.

Subramanian, an Indian journalist, lives and works in the UK. *See also: Following Fish: Travels Around the Indian Coast (2010)*

Read on

Anil's Ghost by Michael Ondaatje (2000); Mosquito by Roma Tearne (2007); Island of a Thousand Mirrors by Nayomi Munaweera (2012); The Story of a Brief Marriage by Anuk Arudpragasam (2016); The Hungry Ghosts by Shyam Selvadurai (2012); Suncatcher by Romesh Gunesekera (2019); Elephant Complex: Travels in Sri Lanka by John Gimlette (2015); Return to Sri Lanka: Travels in a Paradoxical Island by Razeen Sally (2019)

Thailand

Four Reigns by Kukrit Pramoj (1981), translated by Tulachandra

Kukrit's epic, brick-sized novel follows one woman's life from the 1890s to the second world war, spanning the reigns of four kings. At the age of 10, Phloi goes to live in the royal palace in Bangkok with her mother, who serves as a minor courtier. Phloi's eventful life inside and outside the palace – as daughter, sister, wife and mother – reflects the enormous changes taking place in the country. Traditional Siam is buffeted by historic events at home and abroad – a palace revolution, two world wars, Japanese occupation, allied bombing – as it evolves into modern Thailand.

After the absolute monarchs are forced to become constitutional rulers, "the air is thick" with politics. That, along with increasing western influence and the turbulence of the second world war, causes fissures in society that intrude into Phloi's family.

This leisurely paced novel is both intriguing and entertaining. And despite being bathed in conservative nostalgia, it offers a fascinating insight into the country's history and traditions. Four Reigns is regarded as a classic in Thailand and has often been staged and serialised on TV.

Oxford-educated Kukrit – described as a "renaissance man" – was prime minister (preceded and succeeded by his brother), as well as a journalist, author, newspaper proprietor, Hollywood film actor and classical dancer. He died in 1995. *See also: Many Lives (1995), translated by Meredith Borthwick*

Sightseeing by Rattawut Lapcharoensap (2004)

"Pussy and elephants. That's all these people want," says a hotel owner who caters for *farangs* (Thai slang for foreigners). That sets the tone for an east-west culture clash in the opening tale of this lively debut collection of short stories set in contemporary Thailand. It's a fresh, provocative take on the country's beauty and bleakness – without a hint of exoticism.

In the poignant title story, a son and his mother, who is rapidly going blind, go on a trip to see their country as tourists. In Priscilla the Cambodian, a boy learns of the hostility towards migrants. And in the novella-length Cockfighter, a family is almost torn apart by a father's obsession with betting, bird-fighting and getting even with the town bully. The first-person narration in each of the seven stories immediately draws the reader in, whether it's about cultural discord, coming of age and the loss of innocence, small-town corruption or social divisions. The narrators, mostly young Thais, are finding their way in an inequitable and irrational adult world.

An acute observer, Rattawut makes a candid and witty tour guide to the darker side of the "land of smiles". And despite an undercurrent of anger and frustration in the stories, he avoids pamphleteering.

Rattawut, a Thai-American born in Chicago and raised in Bangkok, lives in New York.

A History of Thailand by Chris Baker and Pasuk Phongpaichit (2005)

This accessible history focuses on the economic, social and political forces that shaped contemporary Thailand. Baker and Pasuk reveal how ruling nobles, unfree labourers, Chinese migrants and Buddhism all became part of the mix as the country was transformed from a culturally and linguistically disparate region into a homogenised nation under a strong monarchy. Although Thailand avoided direct colonial rule, it didn't escape foreign machinations. French and British territorial ambitions had to be managed, the second world war brought Japanese occupation, and the US underwrote dictatorship and recruited Thailand as an ally during the cold war.

The Thai military and Washington also oversaw a revival of the monarchy following its partial eclipse in 1932, when it was forced into a constitutional role (today Thailand has severe lese-majesty laws). The authors recount how, over the years, nationalists, army generals, communist guerrillas, businessmen and civil society movements have all attempted to capture the state and bend it to their beliefs. The right, seeking to impose its formula of nation, religion and king, comes up against reformers pushing for a more liberal, democratic state. The battle remains unresolved, as recent military coups attest to.

Baker and Pasuk are a husband-and-wife team: the former taught Asian history at Cambridge University and has lived in Thailand for more than 20 years; the latter teaches at Chulalong-korn University in Bangkok.

Read on

Bangkok Wakes to Rain by Pitchaya Sudbanthad (2019); A Kingdom in Crisis: Thailand's Struggle for Democracy in the Twenty-First Century by Andrew MacGregor Marshall (2014); Jasmine Nights by SP Somtow (1994); The Sad Part Was by Prabda Yoon (2017), translated by Mui Poopoksakul; Bright by Duanwad Pimwana (2019), translated by Mui Poopoksakul; The Politician and Other Stories by Khamsing Srinawk (1973), translated by Domnern Garden and Herbert P Phillips; The Judgment by Chart Korbjitti (1983), translated by Phongdeit Jiangphatthanarkit; A Good True Thai by Sunisa Manning (2020)

Vietnam

The Sorrow of War by Bao Ninh (1990), English version by Frank Palmos from the original translation by Phan Thanh Hao

This rare account of the American war (AKA Vietnam war) by a North Vietnamese army veteran, although fiction, revealed truths to many people inside and outside Vietnam. The main protagonist, Kien – a thinly disguised Bao Ninh himself – is a tortured soul whose sanity is threatened by his brutal experiences during the war. The story begins after the war, with Kien working in an army unit clearing battlefields of rotting corpses. The sites, among them the aptly named Forest of Screaming Souls, bring on hallucinations and nightmares as he's tormented by memories of a decade of war.

Kien battles drunkenness and depression as he struggles to come to terms with his shattered dreams and loss of youth and innocence. To exorcise his demons, he begins to write feverishly about his past and his present – and he tells of a generation of Vietnamese damaged by the war. The novel's raw honesty and intensity carry the reader along as the author reveals not only the sorrow but also the horrors of war.

Bao Ninh fought in the war as part of a youth brigade of whose 500 members only 10 survived. The Sorrow of War is his only published novel. Initially banned by the government, it became a bestseller in Vietnam.

Paradise of the Blind by Duong Thu Huong (1988), translated by Phan Huy Duong and Nina McPherson

Three women struggle to survive in this savage account of Vietnam's Maoist-style land reform of the 1950s and its aftermath. Hang, a young woman, tells of the hardship, chaos and disillusionment the policy sowed, dividing her family and shattering the lives of her mother and aunt.

Forced to leave her village, Hang grew up in Hanoi's slums. Now, in the 1980s, she is an "exported worker" in the Soviet Union – like hundreds of thousands of fellow Vietnamese – because of economic woes at home. In her sadness, she reflects: "No happiness can hold; every life, every dream, has its unravelling." Much of the story is told through flashbacks as Hang takes a long train ride to Moscow to meet her uncle; the same uncle who, as a senior Communist party official, zealously pursued land reform in her village and destroyed the family.

Caught between her mother's unending self-sacrifice and her aunt's deep bitterness, Hang learns she must break free from the past to be able to get on with her life.

Duong Thu Huong, a Communist party member who fought against the US in the war, paid heavily for her disenchantment with the regime. She was expelled from the party, spent time in jail, and has seen her books banned.

See also: Novel Without a Name (1991); Memories of Pure Spring, both translated by Phan Huy Duong and Nina McPherson

Vietnam: Rising Dragon by Bill Hayton (2010)

Hayton's highly readable and informative book is a laudable contribution to understanding contemporary Vietnam. Having worked as a correspondent in the country, he's able to peel back the layers to reveal the political, economic and social forces at work in the country during "a breathtaking period of social change".

The Communist party's *doi moi* (renovation) reforms in 1986 tentatively declared the country open for business. The introduction of capitalism with Vietnamese characteristics – chaotic, corrupt and under party control – has lifted millions out of poverty. But although the economy has grown rapidly, freedoms have not. The party keeps a tight rein on all aspects of life, and beneath the transformation "lurks a paranoid and deeply authoritarian political system".

The get-rich-quick mentality has brought systemic corruption and environmental degradation comparable in some areas, Hayton says, to that caused by the US use of Agent Orange during the war. As for the "monstrous" war, he regrets that discussion about it is suppressed under a policy of "official forgetting", so as not to upset Hanoi's new friends in Washington. As a result,

Vietnamese war veterans are denied a public platform and many are "trapped in voiceless rage".

Hayton, who covered Vietnam for the BBC, was expelled by Hanoi for reporting on dissidents – but that doesn't seem to have dampened his enthusiasm for the country.
See also: The South China Sea: The Struggle for Power in Asia (2014)

Read on

The Mountains Sing by Nguyen Phan Que Mai (2020); The Sympathiser by Viet Thanh Nguyen (2015); The Penguin History of Modern Vietnam by Christopher Goscha (2016); On Earth We're Briefly Gorgeous by Ocean Vuong (2019); The Sacred Willow: Four Generations in the Life of a Vietnamese Family by Duong Van Mai Elliott (1999); The General Retires and Other Stories by Nguyen Huy Thiep (1992), translated by Greg Lockhart

Asia general

The Great Game: On Secret Service in High Asia by Peter Hopkirk (1990)

Hopkirk delivers a ripping yarn of the machinations by imperial Britain and tsarist Russia to dominate central Asia in the 19th century.
See also: Trespassers on the Roof of the World: The Race for Lhasa (1982)

The Silk Roads: A New History of the World by Peter Frankopan (2015)

As global power shifts eastwards, Frankopan's acclaimed, sweeping history highlights the role of trade and cultural exchanges between east and west that shaped the world – and he brings the story up to date with a sibling volume (below).

See also: The New Silk Roads: The Present and Future of the World (2018)

Blood and Silk: Power and Conflict in Modern Southeast Asia by Michael Vatikiotis (2017)

Clear, informative examination of the (often authoritarian) politics and multiple conflicts that bedevil a region better known for its so-called tiger economies.

See also: Lives Between The Lines: A Journey in Search of the Lost Levant (2021)

Read on

The South China Sea: The Struggle for Power in Asia by Bill Hayton (2014); The Light of Asia: A History of Western Fascination with the East by Christopher Harding (2024); How Asia Works: Success and Failure in the World's Most Dynamic Region by Joe Studwell (2013)

Latin America and the Caribbean

Argentina

The Tango Singer by Tomás Eloy Martínez (2004), translated by Anne McLean

Bruno Cadogan, a doctoral student in New York, is having trouble with his dissertation on writer and poet Jorge Luis Borges's essays on the tango. He decides to travel to Buenos Aires in search of inspiration and to track down a disabled, haemophiliac tango singer named Julio Martel, rumoured to be even better than the legendary Carlos Gardel.

Cadogan arrives in the Argentinian capital in 2001, in the midst of financial meltdown and political instability. He pounds the streets of Buenos Aires searching for the elusive singer, who makes unannounced appearances in seemingly random locations across the city. But as he begins to unravel the mystery of Martel's life, Cadogan learns that the tango singer's performances map the city's murky past. Cadogan also develops an obsession with the "The Aleph" – the imaginary point in space that contains the entire universe – as described in an eponymous short story by Borges.

In this vibrant and passionate novel, Martínez meshes fact with fiction to reveal unsavoury events – human trafficking, torture, killings – in the history of "a city where unpunished crimes abound". However, this novel is also a homage to both Buenos Aires and Borges.

Martínez, one of Argentina's best-known journalists and authors, was forced into exile in the 1970s. He went to Venezuela, later moving to the US, and didn't return to live in Argentina until 2006. He died in 2010.

See also: Santa Evita (1995); The Perón Novel (1985), both translated by Helen Lane

My Father's Ghost is Climbing in the Rain by Patricio Pron (2013), translated by Mara Faye Lethem

Patricio Pron's genre-defying novel of a struggle between memory and forgetting focuses on the "dirty war" in the 1970s when the country was under military rule.

The narrator returns to Argentina in 2008 from self-imposed exile in Berlin to be with his dying father. In his parents' house, he finds a trove of newspaper articles and photographs relating to a recent missing-person case, that of 60-year-old Alberto José Burdisso. But the key is material about the disappearance of Alberto's sister, Alicia, decades earlier, under Argentina's murderous military dictatorship. Through it, the son is able to piece together his father's past. He learns that his parents were part of an underground leftwing Peronist group that opposed the military junta, and that some members paid for their audacity with their lives.

The quirky, fragmented telling of the story is challenging in parts, but perseverance pays dividends as the haunting novel excavates the family's – and Argentina's – recent history, with its attendant horrors. "Your father isn't sad that he fought the war," the narrator's mother says, "he's only sad that we didn't win."

In this largely autobiographical tale, the author pays tribute to those in his parents' generation who defied the dictatorship. Pron was born in Argentina in 1975, the year before the "dirty war" began. He now lives in Spain.

See also: Don't Shed Your Tears for Anyone Who Lives on These Streets (2016), translated by Mara Faye Lethem

The Argentina Reader: History, Culture, Politics, edited by Gabriela Nouzeilles and Graciela Montaldo (2002)

An impressive array of articles and documents offers a stellar introduction to this enigmatic country. Once one of the richest nations in the world, Argentina entered the 21st century with its economy in tatters and its politics tarnished by corruption and authoritarianism. The "missteps" that laid the country low are chronicled here.

A wide range of contributors – mostly Argentinians – write on history, society, politics and culture. Ten chapters tell the country's story from the colonial period, through independence in 1810, to the 21st century.

The main focus is on the 20th century, when popular movements spurred the "puzzling political phenomenon" of Peronism and the revolutionary ideals of the 1960s and 1970s. But these were decimated by death squads as Argentina descended into "the bloodiest dictatorship in its history": thousands were tortured and killed under military rule between 1976 and 1983. When democracy finally returned, it came with some unpalatable add-ons – hyperinflation, neoliberal policies and IMF edicts – that shattered Argentinians' standard of living. Although the book runs to almost 600 pages, the easily digestible chapters allow for dipping in and out at leisure. A richer and more eclectic overview of the country and its people would be hard to find.

Argentinian academics Gabriela Nouzeilles and Graciela Montaldo are professors at Princeton University and Columbia University, respectively.

Read on

Kiss of the Spider Woman by Manuel Puig (1976), translated by Thomas Colchie; The Islands by Carlos Gamerro (1998), translated by Ian Barnett; Operation Massacre by Rodolfo Walsh (1957), translated by Daniela Gitlin; Fever Dream by Samanta Schweblin (2014), translated by Megan McDowell; The Dangers of Smoking in Bed by Mariana Enriquez (2009), translated by Megan McDowell; Elena Knows by Claudia Piñero (2007), translated by Frances Riddle; Kamchatka by Marcelo Figueras (2006), translated by Frank Wynne; Resistance by Julián Fuks (2018), translated by Daniel Hahn

Brazil

The Violent Land by Jorge Amado (1943), translated by Samuel Putnam

Amado's novel about the 1920s cacao wars in north-east Brazil is an epic tale of greed, lust, love and murder. Two powerful families, one led by Zinho Badaros and the other by Horacio Silveira, battle over the virgin forest of Sequeiro Grande, which they want to develop as cacao plantations, to increase their wealth and power.

These hard-bitten, wealthy men of the Bahia region – backed by lawyers, guns and money – pursue their land-grabbing through fair means and foul, employing deceit and violence where necessary. Workers flock to the lawless land with dreams of making quick fortunes, but find only harsh regimes on the plantations where the near slave-like conditions bring death and disease. Meanwhile, for the conquistadors of this land "fertilised by blood" it is the best in the world for planting the cacao that, to them, is "worth more than gold".

Amado vividly describes life in the local towns – with their adventurers, assassins, prostitutes and corrupt officials – inspired by his time growing up in the region as the son of a cocoa planter. The Violent Land is reputed to be the greatest novel by Brazil's best-selling author and was his favourite.

A sometime Communist party member, Amado endured prison and exile in the 1930s and 40s. He died in 2001.

See also: Tent of Miracles (1968), translated by Barbara Shelby Merello; Gabriella, Clove and Cinnamon (1958), translated by James L Taylor and William L Grossman; Captains of the Sands (1937), translated by Gregory Rabassa

Bahia Blues by Yasmina Traboulsi (2003), translated by Polly McLean

A short, sharp novel about a group of people who congregate daily in a square in the north-eastern city of Salvador de Bahia. In monologues, the protagonists tell their stories as they go about their daily business, struggling to make a living. The characters, although mostly archetypal, are written with warmth and empathy. Among them are a popcorn vendor, two gay, HIV-positive rent boys, an orphaned prostitute, a bitter, failed writer, and a seven-year-old sweet seller who is already the head of his family. This small community is under the protective eye of Maria Aparecida, an ageing carnival queen.

The arrival of an outsider, Gringa, is a catalyst for change, forcing those in the group to re-examine their lives. Some abandon Bahia, following their dreams – nourished by TV soap operas – to find a better life in the megacities of southern Brazil. But in the big urban world, life can be both hard and harsh. This passionately told tale offers a slice of 21st-century Brazilian life – in Rio's violent, gang-ridden favelas, on São Paulo's anonymous, busy streets and under the brutal regime of Bahia's Canju prison.

Traboulsi, a lawyer of Lebanese and Brazilian parentage, delivers a powerful, gritty and impressive debut novel.

A Death in Brazil: A Book of Omissions by Peter Robb (2003)

Robb's appetite for culinary delights is, fortunately, matched by a thirst for knowledge. He cleverly mixes food with history and politics in a book littered with fascinating digressions. A Death in Brazil is a heady cocktail of history, reportage, memoir and travelogue. Engaging and informative, it often reads like a novel (and a thriller at that).

The book sweeps through 500 years of Brazil's history, from colonisation by the Portuguese, through decades of military dictatorship to working-class hero Luiz Inácio Lula da Silva's winning the presidency in 2003. Robb covers the slavery that lasted longer than anywhere else in the western hemisphere, the destruction of the fugitive slave settlement in Palmares, and the war against the religious community at Canudos. Along the way, he introduces classic Brazilian literary works.

The death of the title is the gruesome killing in 1996 of PC Farias – fixer and bagman to the corrupt president Fernando Collor de Mello (who was forced to resign). But there are many other deaths referenced in the massacres, assassinations and murders in Brazil's turbulent past.

Though Robb paints an affectionate, perceptive portrait of the country, he gives full rein to his anger at the monstrous inequities in Brazilian society. The Australian writer lived for many years in Italy and Brazil, returning to Sydney in the 1990s. *See also: Midnight in Sicily (1996)*

Read on

Brazil: A Biography byLilia M Schwarcz and Heloisa M Starling (2015); Hour of the Star by Clarice Lispector (1977), translated by Benjamin Moser; Crooked Plow by Itamar Vieira Júnior (2019), translated by Johnny Lorenz; An Invincible Memory by João Ubaldo Ribeiro (1989), translated by the author; The Dark Side of Skin by Jefferson Tenório (2024), translated by Bruna Dantas Lobato; Crow Blue by Adriana Lisboa (2010), translated by Alison Entrekin; Heliopolis by James Scudamore (2009); City of God by Paolo Lins (1997), translated by Alison Entrekin; Backlands: The Canudos Campaign (formerly Rebellion in the Backlands) by Euclides da Cunha (1902), translated by Elizabeth Lowe; Beef, Bible and Bullets: Brazil in the Age of Bolsonaro by Richard Lapper (2021); Spilt Milk by Chico Buarque (2009), translated by Alison Entrekin

Chile

The House of the Spirits by Isabel Allende (1982), translated by Magda Bogin

Allende's classic, hugely successful family saga is a masterwork of magic realism. Fusing the personal with the political and fact with fantasy, it retells Chile's recent history through several generations of the Trueba family, ending with a military coup that leads to the death of a president.

The principal protagonist, Esteban Trueba, is used to getting his own way – in his family (as an irascible patriarch), on his farm (as a wealthy landowner), and in the country (as a rightwing senator). "The day we can't get our hands on the ballot boxes before the vote is counted, we're done for," he says. When a socialist candidate finally wins the presidential election, Trueba backs a coup. But in the ferocious denouement that follows, he finds himself sidelined as brutality and terror spiral under the newly installed military regime.

The novel celebrates the spirit and resilience of the Trueba women, which shine through the political tumult and family turbulence in this clever, witty and stunningly assured debut.

Allende's father was a cousin of President Salvador Allende, who was overthrown and died during a military coup in 1973. In 1975, the author fled to Venezuela, and later moved to the US. She has said the book is an "attempt to recreate the country I had lost, the family I had lost".

See also: Of Love and Shadows (1984), translated by Margaret Sayers Peden; A Long Petal of the Sea (2019), translated by Nick Caistor and Amanda Hopkinson

Curfew by José Donoso (1988), translated by Alfred MacAdam

Donoso's engrossing novel spans 24 hours in the stifling and oppressive political atmosphere of 1985 Santiago under General

Augusto Pinochet's military regime. A leftwing singer returns after more than a decade exiled in Paris. His fame now faded and his politics mellowed, Mañungo Vera is no longer the fiery revolutionary he once was. His visit coincides with the death of Matilde Neruda, widow of Pablo, the Nobel prize-winning poet and icon of the Chilean left.

Vera is reacquainted with old friends and comrades as they prepare for the funeral. But, caught out by the curfew, he is forced to spend an eventful night on the streets with his former lover, during which they have a dangerous run-in with her suspected torturer. Donoso paints a harrowing picture of life under the repressive military regime, and shows how negotiating its daily horrors damages both individuals and society. He doesn't shrink from also shining a harsh light on the left, as factions squabble and jockey to gain advantage from the funeral. This intense, introspective tale reflects the political and spiritual decay of the nation after more than a decade of dictatorship.

The author lived abroad for 15 years, returning to Chile in 1982 while Pinochet was still in power. Curfew was the first novel he wrote after his return. He died in 1996.
See also: A House in the Country (1983), translated by David Pritchard with Suzanne Jill Levine

A Nation of Enemies by Pamela Constable and Arturo Valenzuela (1992)

In September 1973, General Augusto Pinochet – with US backing – violently overthrew the elected government of Salvador Allende. In a "spasm of military fury", the regime crushed its perceived foes and began "a reign of professional state terror".

Constable and Valenzuela show how the post-putsch climate of fear and loathing further polarised class and politics, and turned Chile into "a nation of enemies". The military regime allowed the Chicago Boys, US-trained, evangelical free-marketeers, to impose their "shock treatment" on the economy, bringing boom and bust, winners and losers, and exacerbating the divisions in society.

The authors eschew a chronological account of the 17-year dictatorship, instead offering a window into each sector of society through research and interviews with hundreds of Chileans. The ageing and paranoid dictator was finally forced from office after a referendum in which he discovered that he was much less popular than he'd imagined. Pinochet's coup followed around 150 years of constitutional government, and the country is still coming to terms with that aberration.

This is an accessible, balanced and forensic account of how Chile lost and then found its way back to democracy and respect for human rights. Constable was a deputy foreign editor at the Washington Post. Valenzuela is a Chilean-American academic and former US assistant secretary of state.

Read on

By Night in Chile by Roberto Bolaño (2000), translated by Chris Andrews; Ways of Going Home by Alejandro Zambra (2011), translated by Megan McDowell; The Remainder by Alia Trabucco Zerán (2018), translated by Sophie Hughes; The Twilight Zone by Nona Fernández (2016), translated by Natasha Wimmer; My Tender Matador by Pedro Lemebel (2001), translated by Katherine Silver; Humiliation by Paulina Flores (2019), translated by Megan McDowell; The Suicide Museum by Ariel Dorfman (2023)

Colombia

One Hundred Years of Solitude by Gabriel García Márquez (1967), translated by Gregory Rabassa

In the best-known – and perhaps most dazzling – novel to come out of Latin America, Colombia's favourite son takes us on a magic-realist carpet ride through his country's turbulent past. The book's iconic opening sentence is like no other: "Many years later, as he faced the firing squad, Colonel Aureliano Buendía was to remember that distant afternoon when his father took him to discover ice."

Historical fact is liberally mixed with fantasy in a saga that spans six generations of the Buendía family. The Buendías have great strengths as well as fatal flaws, which play out in the rise and fall of the mythical town of Macondo in the South American jungle. Macondo, "an intricate stew of truth and mirages", bears more than a passing resemblance to the author's own home town of Aracataca, near Colombia's Caribbean coast.

In this sweep of history as seen through the eyes of a single family, the country is embroiled in a long-running civil war, causing lives, loves and best-laid plans to be rent asunder. The dizzying chronology – in which time seems to lapse, loop, speed up, slow down or stand still – along with generations of Buendías sharing names and characteristics, gives us history as a story of repetition and return. That keeps readers on their toes in this absorbing, tragicomic novel.

With this book, his magnum opus, the master of magic realism took a giant step towards winning the Nobel prize for literature in 1982. García Márquez died in 2015.

See also: Love in the Time of Cholera (1985), translated by Edith Grossman; Chronicle of a Death Foretold (1981), translated by Gregory Rabassa

Delirium by Laura Restrepo (2004), translated by Natasha Wimmer

Restrepo sets her novel in the drug-fuelled 1980s heyday of cocaine king Pablo Escobar, and uses insanity in one family to reflect the collective insanity of her native Colombia. Aguilar, a grizzled, leftwing literature professor who is reduced to selling dog food to make ends meet, returns from a business trip to find that his beautiful wife, Agustina, has gone mad. In his search for the causes of her delirium, he uncovers secrets and lies from her troubled past.

This complex and captivating novel uses the voices of Agustina, her husband, her father and a former lover – the oddly named Midas McAlister, a flamboyant money-launderer and drug trafficker – to give an account of a Colombia in thrall to narco-capitalism and battered by violence and corruption. The story mostly takes place in the capital, Bogotá, which Aguilar describes as a city "where everyone's at war with everyone else".

Restrepo has a sharp eye for exposing the hypocrisies and class divisions that dog Colombian society, and memorably depicts the period's excesses. Yet, through this morass, the novel – remarkably – ends on a hopeful note.

Journalist and writer Restrepo's involvement in Colombian politics in the 1980s brought death threats, forcing her to spend a number of years exiled in Mexico.

See also: Leopard in the Sun (1999), translated by Stephen A Lytle; The Divine Boys (2017), translated by Carolina De Robertis

Short Walks from Bogotá: Journeys in the New Colombia by Tom Feiling (2012)

Feiling points out that Colombia is the worst place in the world to be a trade unionist, with thousands "disappeared" or murdered since 1985, and that its army is one of the worst human rights abusers in the western hemisphere. Yet the country is Washington's closest ally in Latin America and the biggest recipient of US military aid in the region. Bizarrely, one of the world's most unequal nations is also one of its happiest.

With a book on the cocaine trade and a documentary about Colombia already under his belt, Feiling is well placed to tackle the country's contradictions and unpick its complexities. He finds Colombia trying hard to transform itself after decades of violence and being at the heart of the drugs trade. What was once dubbed a "narco-state" is now one of the region's fastest-growing economies and a darling of foreign investors. Although it hasn't quite segued from "terrorism to tourism", as claimed by hardline former president Álvaro Uribe, there are reasons to be optimistic about the future.

By visiting urban and rural areas once closed off by the violence, talking with Colombians, and maintaining an unflinching eye, the British writer, journalist and film-maker is able to offer us a deft and enlightening introduction to this vibrant country. *See also: The Candy Machine: How Cocaine Took Over the World (2009)*

Read on

Magdalena: River of Dreams by Wade Davis (2020); The Sound of Things Falling by Juan Gabriel Vásquez (2011), translated by Anne McLean; Oblivion: A Memoir by Héctor Abad Faciolince (2006), translated by Anne McLean and Rosalind Harvey; The Vortex by

José Eustasio Rivera (1924), translated by Daniel Hahn and Victor Meadowcroft; The Armies by Evelio Rosero (2007), translated by Anne McLean; Rosario Tijeras by Jorge Franco (1999), translated by Gregory Rabassa; The Bitch by Pilar Quintana (2017), translated by Lisa Dillman; The Lucky Ones By Julianne Pachico (2017)

Cuba

Havana Fever by Leonardo Padura (2009), translated by Peter Bush

It's 2003, and ex-cop Mario Conde – the hard-drinking, heretical anti-hero of Padura's Havana Quartet of crime novels – is now a second-hand book dealer. In his constant search for literary gems, he stumbles across the decaying mansion of a wealthy Cuban who fled the country after the revolution. Inside, Conde discovers a library containing a treasure trove of antique books, watched over by a half-starved brother and sister.

One of the dusty volumes yields up a newspaper cutting about a beautiful bolero singer who disappeared 50 years ago. Conde becomes obsessed with finding out what happened to her. Then one of the library's custodians is murdered. Are the two events linked across the decades? With sleuthing still in the former detective's blood, Conde sets out to crack both cases.

Padura vividly evokes the glamour and sleaze of the 1950s under the Batista dictatorship – when Havana was a mafia-run playground for rich Americans – and the hardships of daily life in post-Soviet Cuba. The Cuban capital is central to the story as Conde's inquiries lead him from the heart of his beloved Havana to its dark and dangerous underbelly. This is crime noir delivered with all the verve of a memorable bolero.

Padura, an investigative journalist-turned-novelist, still lives in the Havana neighbourhood where he grew up.

See also: Havana Red (2005), translated by Peter Bush; Heretics (2013), translated by Anna Kushner

Dreaming in Cuban by Cristina García (1992)

García's bittersweet novel of love, loss and longing, set against the backdrop of the Cuban revolution, tells the story of three generations of women in the Del Pino family who are divided by loyalties and location. Celia, the matriarch, lives in Cuba and loves the island and El Líder (Fidel Castro). Her elder daughter, Lourdes, has fled to the US with her family, embraced the American dream and despises Castro. Meanwhile, Celia's troubled younger daughter, Felicia, seeks solace in the Afro-Cuban religion of santeria.

Most of the "dreaming in Cuban" is done by Celia's New York-based granddaughter, Pilar, who struggles to bring together the fragmented pieces of her Cuban-American identity. The rebellious punk-artist mocks her mother Lourdes's rightwing views and yearns to be with her grandmother to replenish the idealised memories she has of the island that she left as a child. Pilar ultimately engineers a visit to Cuba with her mother for a brief, emotionally charged family reunion, which culminates with the 1980 Mariel exodus of Cubans to the US.

García's lyrical storytelling moves from first to third person, past to present, and Havana to New York. And although the protagonists carry unrealised dreams and frustrated hopes, infusions of humour and magic realism lend the novel an alluring lightness of touch.

Havana-born, New York City-raised García worked as a journalist before writing this, her first novel.

See also: The Aguero Sisters (1997)

Cuba: A New History by Richard Gott (2004)

Gott's rich, comprehensive chronicle of Cuban history sweeps across 500 years, from Spanish colonisation to the present day, with an emphasis on the 20th century. The arrival of the Spaniards led to the indigenous population being decimated, through slaughter and disease. Black slaves were imported to work the sugarcane and tobacco fields, and racism became a constant on the Caribbean island. A long war of independence brought US intervention and a brief occupation in 1898. The nascent Cuban republic was plagued by violence, corruption and persistent US meddling – both military and political. The resentment created, Gott says, "was eventually swept away by Fidel Castro's revolution in 1959".

The revolution put Cuba on the world stage, but its radical nature meant that within months the US had settled on

its overthrow. Washington's trade embargo and backing for
the Bay of Pigs invasion in 1961 resulted in Castro embracing
the Soviets. Gott offers a sharp, balanced analysis of Havana's
domestic and foreign policies, including its attempts to export
the revolution – led by Che Guevara – and military expeditions
to Africa. In the 1990s, the regime overcame an existential crisis,
weathering a harsh economic storm after the USSR's collapse.
In summing up, Gott writes: "Cuba [has] seen off three colonial
powers: Spain, the US and the Soviet Union."

The author, a former Guardian journalist, was present in Bolivia
to identify Guevara's body when he was killed there in 1967.

Read on

Cuban Revelations: Behind the Scenes in Havana by Marc Frank
(2013); Three Trapped Tigers by Guillermo Cabrera Infante
(1967), translated by Donald Gardner and Suzanne Jill Levine;
Che Guevara: A Revolutionary Life by Jon Lee Anderson (1997);
The Mambo Kings Play Songs of Love by Oscar Hijuelos (1989);
Reasons of State by Alejo Carpentier (1976), translated by Francis
Partridge; Telex from Cuba by Rachel Kushner (2008); Havana:
A Subtropical Delirium by Mark Kurlansky (2017); Dirty Havana
Trilogy by Pedro Juan Gutiérrez (1998), translated by Natasha
Wimmer; Cecilia Valdes Or El Angel Hill by Cirilo Villaverde (1882),
translated by Helen Lane

Dominican Republic

The Feast of the Goat by Mario Vargas Llosa (2000), translated by Edith Grossman

Vargas Llosa's taut, edgy, page-turner about the assassination of Rafael LeónidasTrujillo – AKA the Goat – and its blood-soaked aftermath is a masterpiece of historical fiction. Fact and fiction, past and present are entwined to tell of the last days, in 1961, of the dictator who corrupted and brutalised the Dominican Republic over three decades.

Trujillo lusts after power and women – using his secret police to terrorise Dominicans and exercising his droit du seigneur with young girls and his minister's wives. But with some of those close to him, as well as the US and the Catholic church, increasingly alienated, control is slipping from the ailing dictator's grasp.

The story is told from three different perspectives: that of the daughter of a disgraced Trujillista minister, who returns to the country in 1996 after 35 years in self-imposed exile; of the assassins who, while waiting to ambush the dictator on a highway, reflect on what brought them to that point; and of the vainglorious autocrat himself, who believes he rules by divine right.

Trujillo's death doesn't immediately end the nightmare; his cronies unleash ferocious reprisals against the plotters and their families. It does, however, eventually herald the bloody birth of a democratic opening. This powerful tale is a worthy addition to the Latin American literary canon of dictator novels.

The Peruvian author was at the heart of the 1960s Latin American literary "boom". He was awarded the Nobel prize for literature in 2010.

See also: Conversation in The Cathedral(1969), translated by Gregory Rabassa; Harsh Times (2019), translated by Adrian Nathan West

The Brief Wondrous Life of Oscar Wao by Junot Díaz (2007)

Fat, nerdy, sci-fi obsessed Oscar, the son of immigrants to New Jersey, has one overriding ambition: to get laid. A social misfit in the macho Dominican culture he grows up in, Oscar is constantly falling in love with women who don't love him back. He drowns his disappointments in his writing, aiming to be the Dominican Tolkien.

Díaz knits Oscar's best friend Yunior, his beautiful, rebellious sister Lola, his traumatised, truculent mother Belicia, his indomitable great-aunt La Inca and a dark period of Dominican history into his protagonist's comically tragic story. The novel moves between Oscar's coming of age in the 1980s US and his family's fall from grace in the Dominican Republic during the murderous Trujillo regime, which blighted the country from 1930 to 1961. Oscar's grandfather fell foul of the dictatorship and paid a high price – which the family believes to have been the result of a *fukú* (curse) that continues to haunt future generations. It dogs Oscar's mother, forcing her to leave for the US, and then

Oscar himself, following him on his fateful journey back to the Dominican Republic.

Díaz's propulsive, hyper-energetic prose – mixing streetwise American English with Spanish slang – delivers a hilarious, heart-breaking and hugely entertaining book. The Dominican-American author won a richly deserved Pulitzer prize for this, his debut novel.

See also: Drown (1996); This Is How You Lose her (2012)

Why the Cocks Fight: Dominicans, Haitians and the Struggle for Hispaniola by Michele Wucker (1999)

Two very different countries share the Caribbean island of Hispaniola, with little love lost between them. The Dominican Republic and Haiti are divided by language (Spanish and French respectively), culture and skin colour (mixed race and black). Wucker uses the analogy of roosters doing battle in a closed ring – cockfighting is popular in both – to illustrate their fractious relationship; their leaders often inflaming nationalist passions for political gain.

The nadir was reached in 1937, when the Dominican dictator Trujillo ordered his troops to slaughter thousands of Haitians in his country. Poor Haitians continue to toil in near-slave conditions in cane fields across the border in the Dominican Republic, and they and their compatriots face racism and being made scapegoats for Dominican ills.

Since being "discovered" by Columbus in 1492, Dominican territory has played unwilling host to troops from France, Spain, Haiti and the US (twice). Trujillo emerged from the national guard set up during the first US occupation (1916-24). Over some 70 years, he and his protege Joaquin Balaguer repressed Dominicans and stole elections (and money), casting a long shadow over the country.

Wucker's empathetic, anecdotally rich overview of the island braids history with folklore and everyday events to explain past complexities and present contradictions.

The US journalist, commentator and policy analyst has reported from both the Dominican Republic and Haiti.

Read on

In the Time of the Butterflies by Julia Alvarez (1994); The Farming of Bones by Edwidge Danticat (1998); Dominicana by Angie Cruz (2019); The Dominican Republic: A National History by Frank Moya Pons (1994/2010); They Forged the Signature of God by Viriato Sención (1995), translated By Asa Zatz

Guatemala

The Long Night of White Chickens by Francisco Goldman (1992)

A young Guatemalan orphan, Flor de Mayo Puac, is sent to a suburban Boston family as a maid. They decide to adopt her and send her to school, and she becomes a big sister to their son, Roger (Rogerio) Graetz, who is the novel's narrator. Roger – like Goldman himself – has a Jewish-American father and a Guatemalan mother.

Clever, beautiful Flor eventually attends Massachusetts' prestigious Wellesley College. After graduation, she returns to run an orphanage in Guatemala, where she is murdered. She is accused of running an adoption racket, selling Guatemalan orphans – children of people killed by the military – to rich Americans. Roger and his Guatemalan school friend Luis Moya Martinez, now a newspaper columnist, who both loved the enigmatic Flor, embark on a quest to find out who killed her and why. But they're on dangerous ground as they delve into the life and loves of a person who "at times liked to live a double or even a triple life".

Goldman vividly captures the edgy Guatemala of the 1980s, as a bloody civil war rages and death squads operate with impunity. Melding personal with political, the novel segues from coming-of-age tale into whodunnit, history lesson, love story and more. It's a remarkable first book. The author covered the Central American wars as a journalist in the 1980s.

See also: The Art of Political Murder: Who Killed Bishop Gerardi? (2008)

The President by Miguel Angel Ásturias (1946), translated by Frances Partridge

This political satire is an impassioned condemnation of tyranny. Asturias conjures up the nightmarish and paranoid world of a totalitarian regime – a system driven by cruelty, cronyism and corruption. The ruthless president surrounds himself with sycophants and has secret police do his dirty work. His basic tenet is "never to give grounds for hope, and everyone must be kicked and beaten until they realise the fact".

When an army colonel is murdered by a deranged beggar, the president sees an opportunity to manipulate the situation and liquidate his perceived enemies. He tasks his favourite henchman, Miguel Angel Face – "as beautiful and as wicked as Satan" – with setting a trap for a rebellious general. But Angel Face betrays his benefactor, abducts the general's beautiful daughter, and promptly falls in love with her. Tragedy inevitably follows, and reality overlaps with surreality as the regime's arbitrariness and abuse of power are starkly revealed. Although the story takes place in an unnamed Latin American country, it is generally taken to be Guatemala in the early 20th century.

The Guatemalan novelist was a pioneer of both magic realism and the Latin American sub-genre of the dictator novel. He based The President on Manuel Estrada Cabreras, who ruled from 1898 to 1920. Ásturias, who also enjoyed a diplomatic career, won the Nobel prize for literature in 1967. He died in 1974.

See also: Men of Maize (1949), translated by Gerald Martin

Silence on the Mountain: Stories of Terror, Betrayal and Forgetting in Guatemala by Daniel Wilkinson (2004)

On a research visit to Guatemala in 1993, Wilkinson decides to investigate the torching by guerrillas of the landowner's house on a coffee plantation a decade earlier. His inquiries lead him into the country's tortured recent history. As he unravels the mystery of events on La Patria plantation, in Guatemala's western highlands, Wilkinson also tells the broader tale of the 36-year civil war, which ended in 1996.

In 1952, the democratically elected Arbenz government instituted land reform to alleviate the misery of displaced indigenous people and coffee workers. It prompted a CIA-engineered "anti-communist" coup just two years later, heralding Guatemala's long descent into darkness under murderous military regimes. The ensuing civil war left 200,000 dead – more than 90% killed or "disappeared" by the security forces.

Wilkinson focuses on those most affected by the violence. Over many years and visits, he peels away the layers of terror-induced silence and forgetting, and lets people tell their stories – heartbreaking accounts of violence, betrayals and massacres. Ultimately, the most deafening silence is Washington's, during its decades-long support for some of the worst human rights violators in the Americas.

Wilkinson's eye for detail, doggedness and storytelling skills make his book both engaging and enlightening. The New

York-based author, a lawyer at Human Rights Watch, served on Guatemala's post-conflict truth commission in the 1990s.

Read on

I, Rigoberta Menchú by Rigoberta Menchú (1983), translated by Ann Wright; Bitter Fruit: The Story of the American Coup in Guatemala by Stephen Schlesinger and Stephen Kinzer (1982); Harsh Times by Mario Vargas Llosa (2019), translated by Adrian Nathan West; The Guatemala Reader: History, Culture, Politics, edited by Greg Grandin et al (2011); Trout Belly Up by Rodrigo Fuentes (2016), translated by Ellen Jones; Final Silence by Ronald Flores (2001), translated by Gavin O'Toole

Haiti

The Dew Breaker by Edwidge Danticat (2004)

Danticat's novel shuttles between 1960s Haiti and present-day New York as it tells the story of a "Dew Breaker". It's the name given to torturers during the repressive regime of François "Papa Doc" Duvalier, who take victims away "before dawn, as the dew is settling on the leaves". Nine chapters, each of which reads like a short story on its own, provide fragments of the Dew Breaker's life as seen through the eyes of his family and his victims. These fractured vignettes draw the reader into a larger, more complex tale.

The Dew Breaker is now hiding from his bloody past, working as a barber in Brooklyn. But every day he faces the threat of being recognised by one of his victims and exposed for what he once was. In the novel's final chapter, the disparate stories satisfyingly come together as we meet the Dew Breaker preparing for his final killing before leaving Haiti. This clever and powerful novel shows how both hunter and prey – who are seeking new lives in the US – find their present and future circumscribed by an ugly past. Three victims drink a toast to "the terrible days behind us and the uncertain ones ahead".

Danticat was born in Haiti and moved to the US when she was 12. In the acknowledgements, she writes: "For my father, who, thank goodness, is not in this book."
See also: The Farming of Bones (1998); Everything Inside (2019); Krik? Krak! (1995)

The Comedians by Graham Greene (1966)

Greene's classic tragicomedy is set in Haiti during the era of Papa Doc Duvalier and his menacing secret police, the Tontons Macoute. Three men meet on a boat headed for the Haitian capital, Port-au-Prince: the world-weary Brown, the narrator, who owns a hotel in the capital; the idealistic but naive Smith, a former US presidential candidate; and Jones, a charming conman with a fabricated past. These flawed human beings are the comedians of the title, whose fates become intertwined amid Haiti's corruption and violence.

Brown's life becomes increasingly complicated and fraught with danger after the suicide of a government minister in his hotel's swimming pool, his rekindling of an affair with an ambassador's wife, and getting caught up in Jones's foolhardy escapades. Though Duvalier never appears in the novel, he casts a long shadow over events. In a dig at US cold-war policy of often supporting Latin American dictators, we are reminded that the Haitian strongman is a "bulwark against communism", sustained by aid from Washington.

Greene vividly evokes the fear and loathing in Duvalier's Haiti, but his elegantly written black comedy-cum-political thriller allows hope to flicker in the darkness. After the novel's publication, the dictator was furious and banned both the British writer and his book. Greene died in 1991.

Farewell, Fred Voodoo: A Letter from Haiti by Amy Wilentz (2013)

Wilentz's Letter from Haiti is actually a warts-and-all love letter to the country. After Haiti's devastating earthquake in 2010, she is drawn back to the nation she has written about for many years. On arrival, she finds humanitarian aid groups "fighting for a piece of Haitian action", leading her to question their motives – and her own.

Wilentz embarks on a vigorous, intensely personal quest to better understand the country and its people, unafraid to challenge received wisdom and tell inconvenient truths. Along the way, she reveals Haiti's beauty as well as its ugliness through personal stories, politics, culture and its tortured history. Home to "the first and last successful slave revolution in history", Haiti became the world's first black-led republic. But it was made to pay a crippling price for its audacity by France – the colonial master – and the US, from which it has never recovered.

She argues that Haiti and its people – Fred Voodoo is the old, politically incorrect term for the man on the street – need to be understood on their own terms, rather than through western misconceptions and prejudices. Her intimate knowledge along with her acerbic and energetic prose make Wilentz the perfect guide through the country's "post-apocalyptic dystopia".

The US journalist has closely followed Haiti's fortunes since the end of the Duvalier regime in the 1980s.

Read on

God Loves Haiti by Dimitry Elias Léger (2015); Masters of the Dew by Jacques Roumain (1944), translated by Langston Hughes and Mercer Cook; Haiti: The Aftershocks of History by Laurent Dubois (2012); Black Spartacus: The Epic Life of Toussaint Louverture by Sudhir Hazareesingh (2020); Bonjour Blanc: A Journey Through Haiti by Ian Thompson (1992)

Jamaica

A Brief History of Seven Killings by Marlon James (2014)

The title of James's polyphonous, prize-winning novel is misleading: it's not brief – running to 700 pages – and the body count surpasses seven. Set around a real incident, the attempted assassination of Bob Marley in December 1976 by gunmen who attacked his Kingston mansion, it's an unflinching, foul-mouthed portrayal of Jamaica's social turbulence and political turmoil from the 1970s to the 1990s. It's been likened to putting a blood-spattered Tarantino film on the page. Gang warfare and drug-running are rife, and as the leftwing People's National party and conservative Jamaican Labour party jockey for political power, their armed thugs roam the streets.

Among the vast array of characters given voice are gang lords, hitmen, politicians, CIA agents, groupies and journalists. Although the story swirls around the reggae superstar, Marley himself remains on the margins, referred to as The Singer. The sprawling tale is inventive, audacious and hugely ambitious, and alongside the graphic sex and violence runs a river of dark humour. It's an extraordinary construct. However, the multi-person narrative, plot presentation and Jamaican patois make the novel dizzyingly complex – and a challenging read, which gets easier as the characters become more familiar.

A Brief History, James's third novel, won the 2015 Man Booker prize. The author, Jamaican born and raised, now lives in St Paul, Minnesota.

See also: *The Book of Night Women* (2009); *John Crow's Devil* (2005)

Here Comes the Sun by Nicole Dennis-Benn (2016)

Dennis-Benn's accomplished debut novel of love and betrayal in 1990s Jamaica centres on a family of three black women living in a poor village outside Montego Bay. Each struggles with her own demons, which is reflected in the troubled dynamics of this dysfunctional family. With the women's fortunes tethered to the tourist trade, Here Comes the Sun shines a light on the dark side of paradise, examining racism, classism, sexism and homophobia.

Beautiful, driven, 30-year-old Margot works at the front desk of a resort hotel, harbouring dreams of running it one day. Having learned early in life that sex can be traded for benefits, she uses this to pay for her sister Thandi's education, to ensure the teenager won't follow in her footsteps. Their bitter, single mother Delores, who sells trinkets to tourists, has a fractious relationship with her elder daughter, but they both see investment in Thandi (seeing her perhaps becoming a doctor) as their ticket out of poverty. "Can't wait to leave dis godforsaken place," Margot says. "This is no paradise. At least not for us." When the tourist industry's development threatens their community, it brings an unexpected denouement. The vividly drawn characters, vibrant prose and slow burn of painful revelations make this a novel to be savoured.

Dennis-Benn grew up in Jamaica and now lives in New York. *See also: Patsy (2019)*

The Dead Yard: A Story of Modern Jamaica by Ian Thomson (2009)

Before Thomson sets out to travel across the island and write about it, an elderly Jamaican upbraids him, saying: "You visitors are always getting it wrong. Either it's golden beaches or its guns, guns, guns. Is there nothing in between?" In his patchwork portrait of the country, Thomson – by speaking to a cross section of Jamaicans – does reveal an in-between. But there's no ignoring the crime and violence in one of the world's most dangerous places.

Jamaican sugar and slavery enriched the British, but left an ugly legacy, entrenching violence along with social and racial divisions. The colonial power's malign influence has been followed by that of the US – with its economic stranglehold, insatiable appetite fuelling the drugs trade, and American guns dropping into Kingston "like mangoes off a tree". Jamaican elites, too, have ill-served their country, sanctioning corruption and political violence. In the more than half century since independence in 1962, the hopes for a better, fairer Jamaica have not been met.

Thomson's well-researched book seeks to explain the malaise that afflicts this "corrupted Eden". Part history, part travelogue, it teems with fascinating insights and observations, exposing the gritty underbelly that tourists who flock to Jamaica for reggae, rum, sun and sex never see. The British journalist's book is a must-read for anyone interested in this beautiful, bedevilled country.
See also: Bonjour Blanc: A Journey Through Haiti (1992)

Read on

Augustown by Kei Miller (2016); The Long Song by Andrea Levy (2010); The Sugar Barons: Family, Corruption, Empire and War by Matthew Parker (2011); How To Love a Jamaican: Stories by Alexia Arthurs (2018); A Tall History of Sugar by Curdella Forbes (2019); The True History of Paradise by Margaret Cezair-Thompson (1999); A House for Miss Pauline by Diana McCaulay (2025); What a Mother's Love Don't Teach You by Sharma Taylor (2022)

Mexico

The Years With Laura Díaz by Carlos Fuentes (1999), translated by Alfred MacAdam

An epic novel that uses one extraordinary woman's life and loves to sweep through 100 years of Mexican history. The female protagonist, Laura Díaz – daughter, sister, wife, mother, lover – comes of age during the long, bloody Mexican revolution in the early 20th century. The execution of her half-brother Santiago (one of four generations of Santiagos in the novel) by firing squad at the start of the revolution launches her political journey.

Laura witnesses, chronicles, discusses or participates in all of the country's seminal political and cultural events of the 20th century, through to the early 1970s. Real-life luminaries such as artists Diego Rivera and his wife Frida Kahlo are also woven into the rich tapestry of Laura's life. Fuentes's grand project encompasses Mexico's political upheavals, its union movement, the Spanish civil war, the Holocaust, McCarthyism and the massacre of students in Mexico City on the eve of the 1968 Olympics (Laura's grandson, another Santiago, is one of the victims). Its intelligence, emotional power and bold ambition make this a memorable book.

Diplomat, Harvard professor and one of Mexico's most famous writers and polemicists, Fuentes was often mentioned as a Nobel prize contender, but he never won. He died in 2012.

See also: The Death of Artemio Cruz (1962); Where the Air Is Clear (1958), both translated by Sam Hileman; The Old Gringo (1985), translated by Margaret Sayers Peden

Down the Rabbit Hole by Juan Pablo Villalobos (2011), translated by Rosalind Harvey

In Villalobos's small but perfectly formed debut novel, reality and surreality entwine in a darkly comic tale that offers a fresh take on Mexico's nasty narco-wars. Tochtli ("rabbit" in the indigenous Nahuatl language), the precocious, seven-year-old narrator, tells us about his life as the son of a drug kingpin called Yolcaut ("rattlesnake" in Nahuatl). They live in an isolated and well-guarded palace ("the thing is we have a lot of money. A huge amount"), where the boy's every whim is indulged, but he is lonely. He knows only "13 or 14 people ... [But] if I counted dead people, I'd know more".

Tochtli has a passion for hats, samurai, guillotines – and Liberian pygmy hippopotamuses. He reads the dictionary every night, and among the words he likes to use are "pathetic", "devastating", "disastrous" and "sordid". His father doesn't shield him from the ugliness of the drug world, resulting in the child being chillingly well-versed in matters relating to bullets, knives and getting rid of dead bodies. "I think at the moment my life is a little bit sordid. Or pathetic," he says.

Although easily devoured in one sitting, this clever little book is to be contemplated at length afterwards.

Mexico-born Villalobos lived in Spain (where he wrote this novel), and then in Brazil before returning to Spain.
See also: Quesadillas (2013); I'll Sell you a Dog (2014)), both translated by Rosalind Harvey

Mexico: Democracy Interrupted by Jo Tuckman (2012)

In her well-informed overview of Mexico today, Tuckman argues that the country missed a chance to fully embrace democracy after the oxymoronic Institutional Revolutionary party (PRI) was voted out in 2000 after 70 years in power. The rightwing National Action party (PAN), in its subsequent 12 years of running the country, failed to deliver on the hopes it had raised for more transparent and participatory governance, beyond political plurality and generally free and fair elections.

Tuckman investigates the key factors of Mexican life and the challenges the country faces: a savagely violent drugs war (and the US role in it); a flawed judicial system; rampant corruption; poverty and extreme inequality; racism; and environmental degradation. She also examines the infighting that has stymied the ambitions of the left (although post-publication of her book centre-left candidates won the 2018 and 2024 presidential elections), as well as the role played by the church.

History, personal stories and political analysis are interwoven to reveal what makes this fascinating and diverse country tick. Despite some seemingly intractable problems, she sees reasons to be optimistic, with brave, spirited citizens and sections of the media stepping up to do battle for a better future.

Tuckman, who died in 2020, was the Guardian's Mexico correspondent, and lived in and reported on the country for more than 10 years.

Read on

Narcoland: The Mexican Drug Lords and Their Godfathers by Anabel Hernández (2010), translated by Iain Bruce with Lorna Scott Fox; Prayers for the Stolen by Jennifer Clement (2013); Fifth Sun: A New History of the Aztecs by Camilla Townsend (2019); Signs Preceding the End of the World by Yuri Herrera (2009), translated by Lisa Dillman; Hurricane Season by Fernanda Melchor (2017), translated by Sophie Hughes; The Labyrinth of Solitude by Octavio Paz (1950), translated by Lysander Kemp; Pedro Páramo by Juan Rulfo (1955), translated by Margaret Sayers Peden; The Underdogs: A Novel of the Mexican Revolution by Mariano Azuela (1915), translated by Sergio Waisman; The Savage Detectives by Roberto Bolaño (1998), translated by Natasha Wimmer

Nicaragua

Bernardo and the Virgin by Silvio Sirias (2005)

Sirias's novel is based on a true story: the claim in 1980 by a poor tailor-cum-sacristan in a small Nicaraguan town to have communicated with the Virgin Mary, who instructs him to spread a message of peace and prayer. With Bernardo Martínez at its heart, the story – as seen through the eyes of the different narrators who relate the tale – sweeps across decades of Nicaragua's 20th-century history, from the long years under the Somoza family dictatorship to the 1979 Sandinista revolution, its electoral defeat in 1990 and beyond.

The acceptance or otherwise of Bernardo's account becomes highly politicised during the Sandinista years as the revolutionaries clash with the conservative Roman Catholic church, and the seer is whirled into the storm. Devout and humble Bernardo, "a simple man [with] a good heart", yearns to become a priest but is blocked by the church hierarchy because of his lowly status. Mary's apparition provides a mystical force that guides him through the challenges he faces.

Sirias skilfully crafts his protagonist's character and inner struggles as the story weaves in Nicaraguan culture and traditions in redolent prose that is both engaging and propulsive. When the author met Bernardo in 1999, he says: "I became certain I had finally found the perfect vehicle for the panoramic tale I wanted to tell." The author grew up in the US and Nicaragua, and now lives in Panama.

See also: Meet Me Under the Ceiba (2009)

To Bury Our Fathers: A Novel of Nicaragua by Sergio Ramírez, translated by Nick Caistor (1977)

Set during the Somoza autocracy, this novel of resistance and revenge tells personal stories within the broader canvas of a country in upheaval between 1930 and 1960. A motley cast of characters graces the narrative, from National Guardsmen to guerrillas, and presidential candidates to prostitutes.

Former regime loyalists who decide to take up arms against the dictatorship find their rebellions ruthlessly suppressed. Meanwhile, the unctious Col Catalino López remains faithful to the Somozas and commits atrocities in the service of his masters, torturing dissidents. Some of his victims manage to escape into exile in Guatemala. As the exiles bide their time abroad, an opportunity for retribution presents itself when Col López visits Guatemala for a state funeral. Three former rebels manage to lure the corpulent colonel to a brothel for a final reckoning.

The narrative shuffles back and forth in time, which makes for a challenging read. Helpfully, a summary of the main lines of the story is introduced at the beginning of the novel and a chronological timeline presented at the end.

Ramírez, a keen observer of (and protagonist in) his nation's history, wrote this novel in neighbouring Costa Rica during his exile by the Somoza regime. He later served as Nicaragua's vice-president, from 1985 to 1990, under the Sandinista government led by Daniel Ortega. Ructions among the Sandinistas saw him forced into exile once again, in 2021.

See also: Dead Men Cast No Shadows (2023), translated by Daryl R Hague; Margarita, How Beautiful the Sea, translated by Michael B Miller (1998); Divine Punishment, translated by Nick Caistor (1988)

The Country Under My Skin: A Memoir of Love and War by Gioconda Belli, translated by Kristina Cordero with the author (2002)

The Nicaraguan poet and author's revelatory memoir of revolution and romance delivers a frank, insider account of the Sandinista uprising that overthrew the country's US-backed dictatorship in 1979. Through personal narrative and political history she chronicles the struggle against the Somoza regime and the subsequent rise and fall of the Sandinista government. Although she belonged to an upper-class family, Belli's growing awareness of the injustices that blight Nicaragua led her to join the young revolutionaries. She acted as a courier, running guns, carrying money and gathering information.

A who's who of leading Nicaraguan revolutionaries traverses the pages of the book as she juggled risk-taking and romantic entanglements, militancy and motherhood. When state surveillance got too close, she was forced into exile in Costa Rica, from where she continued to work with the Sandinistas – returning the day after the revolutionary triumph in July 1979. Not long after, the then US president, Ronald Reagan, deployed an economic embargo, CIA sabotage and armed counterrevolutionaries, the Contras, in an effort to destroy the Sandinistas.

Belli held senior offices under the revolutionary government, but eventually became disillusioned with the leadership's patriarchal tendencies and increasingly rigid stance under US pressure. And when the Sandinistas lost the 1990 election, she left for a new life and a new love in the US.

See also:The Inhabited Woman, translated by Kathleen March (1988)

Read on

Blood of Brothers: Life and War in Nicaragua by Stephen Kinzer (1991); The Jaguar Smile: A Nicaraguan Journey by Salman Rushdie (1987); A Flag for Sunrise by Robert Stone (1981); Nicaragua: Emerging From the Shadow of the Eagle by Thomas W Walker and Christine J Wade (sixth edition, 2016); Fire from the Mountain:

The Making of a Sandinista by Omar Cabezas (1985), translated by Kathleen Weaver

Peru

Conversation in The Cathedral by Mario Vargas Llosa (1969), translated by Gregory Rabassa

Vargas Llosa's ambitious novel paints a portrait of power and politics in Peru under the dictatorship of General Manuel Odría in the 1950s. Santiago Zavala, a young journalist, bumps into Ambrosio Pardo, his wealthy father's former chauffeur, and they go to a rundown bar in Lima (The Cathedral of the title) to talk about old times. Santiago is estranged from his family, rejecting their upper middle-class values and his father Don Fermín's shady business dealings and rightwing politics. Ambrosio, on the contrary, admires Don Fermín and served him well.

Through their reminiscences they tell the story of the country during those dark years. "At what precise moment had Peru fucked itself up?" asks Santiago on the opening page. Vargas Llosa builds the story around their hours-long conversation, linking it with other characters and conversations. The interlacing of dialogues between different narrators speaking at different times can be tricky, but persistence pays off. The novel is a powerful exploration of repression, corruption and hypocrisy, along with the ugly prejudices of race and class.

Vargas Llosa, one of Latin America's best-known authors, ran for Peru's presidency in 1990. He lost, and so was able to concentrate on his writing rather than on running the country. Twenty years later, aged 74, he won the Nobel prize for literature. *See also: The Discreet Hero (2015); Death in the Andes (1993), both translated by Edith Grossman; The Green House (1966), translated by Gregory Rabassa; The Feast of the Goat (2000), translated by Edith Grossman*

Red April by Santiago Roncagliolo (2006), translated by Edith Grossman

This chilling political thriller is set in the provincial town of Ayacucho in 2000, in the month leading up to Holy Week. Félix Chacaltana Saldívar, an eccentric, mother-obsessed prosecutor, newly returned to his hometown from the capital, Lima, is asked to investigate a series of brutal murders. Is a serial killer on the loose or is a resurgence of the Maoist-inspired Shining Path (Sendero Luminoso) guerrillas to blame? But the savage, two-decade Senderista insurgency that claimed 70,000 lives has been declared officially over. "In this country, there is no terrorism, by orders from the top," a senior military officer tells Chacaltana.

The lines between good and evil blur as civilians are caught between Shining Path terror and the harsh military response. Amid the violence, the state is making preparations to rig the impending presidential election. The prosecutor finds himself out of his depth as the murders get ever closer to him. "All the people I talk to die," Chacaltana observes, as the twist-filled plot careens towards its edge-of-seat ending.

Roncagliolo excavates the dark side of his country's political and cultural turbulence under the Fujimori regime, nailing entrenched corruption, impunity and racism in Peruvian society. That said, the riveting story is served up with irony and black humour. The Peruvian writer, journalist and scriptwriter now lives in Spain.

See also: Hi, This Is Conchita: And Other Stories (2013), translated by Edith Grossman

The Conquest of the Incas by John Hemming (1970)

Hemming's account of how a small band of greedy, god-fearing adventurers destroyed a civilisation is a superb work of history. His impressive scholarship and fluid prose tell an extraordinary tale of courage and cruelty, vividly describing the intrigue, treachery and slaughter that took place as Francisco Pizarro's conquistadors went about their brutish business.

The Spaniards, a mere 168 men, arrived at a time of civil wars and unrest among the native peoples, who were also decimated by the European disease of smallpox – leaving the once-mighty Inca empire weakened. On top of that, Spanish horses, weapons and armour gave the invaders superiority over the native forces.

The book focuses on the 40 years between the initial invasion in 1532 and the execution of the last emperor, Túpac Amaru. Although Hemming remains scrupulously impartial, it's hard not to feel sympathy for the Incas in the unequal struggle between the old and new worlds.

The Spaniards' subjugation and exploitation of the indigenous people shapes the hierarchical Peru of today, which continues to grapple with their legacy. Despite that, as Hemming points out, the Quechua-speaking population has "survived with its language and many of its customs unchanged", and forms a majority in the country.

Hemming, a Canadian-born British writer and explorer, has travelled widely in and written extensively on South America. *See also: Tree of Rivers: The Story of the Amazon (2008)*

Read on

The Peru Reader: History, Culture, Politics, edited by Orin Starn, Carlos Iván Degregori and Robin Kirk (2005); At Night We Walk in Circles by Daniel Alarcón (2013); The Blue Hour by Alonso Cueto (2005), translated by Frank Wynne; The Word of The Speechless: Selected Stories by Julio Ramón Ribeyro (1974/2019), translated by Katherine Silver; Deep Rivers by José María Arguedas (1958), translated by Frances Horning Barraclough; A World for Julius by Alfredo Bryce Echenique (1970), translated by Dick Gerdes

Venezuela

Doña Barbara by Rómulo Gallegos (1929), translated by Robert Malloy

Set in the 1920s, this is an epic tale of the struggle between city and country, civilisation and barbarism, good and evil. Gallegos's novel, considered a Latin American classic, is a paean to the Venezuelan *llano* (plains) and plainsmen. "The plain is at once lovely and fearful," he writes. "It holds, side by side, beautiful life and hideous death. The latter lurks everywhere, but no one fears it."

Santos Luzardo returns from studying in Caracas to reclaim the family ranch in the rural state of Apure, only to discover that much of the land and cattle have been stolen by his cousin, the beautiful and bewitching Doña Barbara. She holds sway in this untamed and lawless region of ranchers, cowboys and rustlers. Santos decides to confront her, and to struggle for justice "in the vast stronghold of violence". But he is hobbled at every turn by the venality of government officials, who are in thrall to the manipulative mistress of the plains. The ensuing battle sees blood spilled and magic and seduction deployed as the novel's lush, lyrical prose casts its own spell on the reader.

Gallegos was Venezuela's first democratically elected president, in 1948, but was overthrown by a military coup within months and went into exile. On his return 10 years later, he was elected a senator for life. He died in 1969.

Doña Iñés vs Oblivion by Ana Teresa Torres (1992), translated by Gregory Rabassa

Torres's magic-realist novel is seen as Venezuela's answer to neighbouring Colombia's One Hundred Years of Solitude. Doña Iñés Villegas y Solórzano, the irascible, aristocratic matriarch of a plantation-owning family, recounts their saga over 300 years, from the early 18th to the late 20th century.

Although her focus is on a bitter family dispute carried through generations – an attempt to reclaim land her now dead husband bequeathed to the son he had with a slave woman – Doña Iñes weaves her story into an idiosyncratic history of Venezuela. That history is rife with political and natural upheaval: slave rebellions, the war of independence from Spain, civil war between liberals and conservatives, dictatorships, and finally democracy, not to mention earthquakes and floods. She sweeps in the exploits of real historical figures, such as the independence leader Simón Bolivar and the dictator Juan Vicente Gómez.

The matriarch dies in 1780 but her ghost continues to narrate the tale until finally, in 1985, a direct descendant – Francisco Villaverde – arrives at a happy resolution of the case. The novel's large cast of characters and Doña Iñes's ramblings can sometimes be frustrating, but rich detail and engaging prose help to carry the story along.

Caracas-born Torres worked as a clinical psychologist for more than two decades before taking up writing full-time.

Comandante: The Life and Legacy of Hugo Chávez by Rory Carroll (2013)

Hugo Chávez came to prominence when, as a young lieutenant colonel in 1992, he led a failed coup against the country's sclerotic ruling elite. Following two years in jail, a dramatic change of fortune swept the once poor plainsman into the presidential palace in the 1999 elections, upending the political system. To the poor, dark-skinned, working-class people who invested their hopes in him, the new president promised improved health and education, a path out of poverty, and a voice in government. For a time he succeeded, particularly when benefiting from record oil revenues, and his popularity soared. He won a series of elections, maintaining his hold on power until his death from cancer in 2013.

However, Carroll notes, Chávez was a "masterful politician who happened to be a bad manager". A concentration of power in one capricious man, economic mismanagement, over-dependence on oil, turning a blind eye to corruption, soaring crime rates and US antipathy (including tacit support for a failed coup in 2002) all contributed, eventually, to stymie his socialist Bolivarian revolution. Although Chávez was no dictator, he became something of an "elected autocrat" and to this day remains an immensely polarising figure, both loved and loathed. This vividly detailed and keenly observed account paints an illuminating portrait of the wily, wilful and charismatic comandante.

Carroll, the Guardian's former Latin America correspondent, was based in Caracas between 2006 and 2012.

Read on

Venezuela: What Everyone Needs to Know by Miguel Tinker Salas (2015); Iphigenia: (The Diary of a Young Lady Who Wrote Because She Was Bored) by Teresa de la Parra (1924), translated by Bertie Acker; Simpatía by Rodrigo Blanco Calderón (2020), translated by Noel Hernández González and Daniel Hahn; The Last Days of El Comandante by Alberto Barrera Tyszka (2019), translated by Rosalind Harvey and Jessie Mendez Sayer; It Would Be Night in Caracas by Karina Sainz Borgo (2019), translated by Elizabeth Bryer

Latin America and the Caribbean general

Open Veins of Latin America: Five Centuries of the Pillage of a Continent by Eduardo Galeano (1971), translated by Cedric Belfrage

Galeano's classic work, a sweeping, angry denunciation of the looting and exploitation of the region over 500 years, is a superb introduction to Latin America.

See also: Children of the Days: A Calendar of Human History (2012); Mirrors: Stories Of Almost Everyone (2008), both translated by Mark Fried; Genesis: Memory of Fire, Volume 1 (2005), translated by Cedric Belfrage

Everyone Who Is Gone Is Here: The United States, Central America, and the Making of a Crisis by Jonathan Blitzer (2024)

A meticulously researched and masterfully written book that drills into the recent history of the US's murky intervention in Central America and its impact on the current immigration crisis.

Bolívar: The Epic Life of the Man Who Liberated South America by Marie Arana (2014)

An engaging and erudite biography of the greatest liberator of the continent from Spanish rule, who is still revered today.

See also: Silver, Sword and Stone: The Story of Latin America in Three Extraordinary Lives (2019)

Read on

The Penguin History of Latin America by Edwin Williamson (1992/2009); Red Heat: Conspiracy, Murder and the Cold War in the Caribbean by Alex Von Tunzelmann (2011); Empire's Crossroads: A History of the Caribbean from Columbus to the Present Day by Carrie Gibson (2014); Gold, Oil, and Avocados: A Recent History of Latin America in Sixteen Commodities by Andy Robinson (2021)

Acknowledgements

Thanks to Steve Sklair for helping me to see the wood and the trees; to Lucy Lamble and Liz Ford for enabling an idea to come to fruition; to Rajan Bhatia for passing along a passion for nonfiction; to Charlotte Thompson for tying up loose ends. And a big thank you to the authors, translators and publishers of the books listed here, without whom, of course, my book couldn't have been written – and I wouldn't have learned so much.

Index

PUSHPINDER KHANEKA